WILD NIGHTS

Kim Addonizio has been called one of America's 'most provocative and edgy poets'. Her collection *Tell Me* was a finalist for the National Book Award. Her first UK publication, *Wild Nights: New & Selected Poems*, was published by Bloodaxe in 2015. A new collection, *Mortal Trash*, is forthcoming from W.W. Norton in 2016.

As well as six other poetry collections, Addonizio has published two books on writing poetry, *The Poet's Companion* (with Dorianne Laux) and *Ordinary Genius: A Guide for the Poet Within*; two novels, *Little Beauties* and *My Dreams Out in the Street*; and the story collections *In the Box Called Pleasure* and *The Palace of Illusions*. Her awards include two NEA Fellowships, a Guggenheim Fellowship, and the John Ciardi Lifetime Achievement Award. She has also been a presenter for BBC radio. She divides her time between New York and the San Francisco Bay Area and plays harmonica with Nonstop Beautiful Ladies, a word/music performance group.

For more information, go to www.kimaddonizio.com.

KIM ADDONIZIO

WILD NIGHTS

NEW & SELECTED POEMS

BLOODAXE BOOKS

First published 2015 by
Bloodaxe Books Ltd,
Eastburn,
South Park,
Hexham,
Northumberland NE46 1BS.

www.bloodaxebooks.com
For further information about Bloodaxe titles
please visit our website or write to
the above address for a catalogue.

Supported by
**ARTS COUNCIL
ENGLAND**

Cover design: Neil Astley & Pamela Robertson-Pearce.

Printed in Great Britain by Bell & Bain Limited, Glasgow, Scotland, on
acid-free paper sourced from mills with FSC chain of custody certification.

ACKNOWLEDGEMENTS

This edition includes poems selected from these books by Kim Addonizio: *The Philosopher's Club* (BOA Editions, 1994), *Tell Me* (BOA Editions, 2000), *What Is This Thing Called Love* (W.W. Norton & Company, 2004), *Lucifer at the Starlite* (W.W. Norton & Company, 2009), and *My Black Angel: Blues Poems and Portraits* (Stephen F. Austin University Press, 2014), with the permission of BOA Editions in the case of *Tell Me* and of Stephen F. Austin University Press for *My Black Angel*.

The *New Poems* are previously uncollected. Acknowledgements are due to the editors of the following publications in which some of these first appeared: *American Poetry Review* ('Sleep Stage'), *Catamaran Literary Review* ('Here Be Dragons'), *Fifth Wednesday* ('Divine'), *Five Points* ('Plastic'), *Great River Review* ('Last Lights'), *Los Angeles Review* ('Dream the Night My Brother Dies', 'Pareidolia'), *Poetry* ('Lives of the Poets'), *Poetry London* ('The Givens'), *Poetry Review* ('Party', 'Prosody Pathetique', 'White Flower, Red Flower'), *PoetsArtists* ('Candy Heart Valentine'), *Psychology Tomorrow* ('Florida'), *River Styx* ('Idioms for Rain'), and *Willow Springs* ('Postmodern Romance: Internet Dating').

'Divine' also appeared in *Best American Poetry 2013*. 'Darkening, Then Brightening' was a Poem-A-Day selection from The Academy of American Poets.

CONTENTS

from **TELL ME** (2000)

from **MY BLACK ANGEL: BLUES POEMS AND PORTRAITS** (2014)

New Poems

(2015)

Lives of the Poets

One stood among the violets
listening to a bird. One went to the toilet
and was struck by the moon. One felt hopeless
until a trumpet crash, and then lo,
he became a diamond. I have a shovel.
Can I turn it into a poem? On my stove
I'm boiling some milk thistle.
I hope it will turn into a winged thesis
before you stop reading. Look, I'm topless!
Listen: approaching hooves!
One drowned in a swimming pool.
One removed his shoes
and yearned off a bridge. One lives
with Alzheimer's in a state facility, spittle
in his white beard. It
turns out words are no help.
But here I am with my shovel
digging like a fool
beside the spilth and splosh
of the ungirdled sea. I can't stop.
The horses are coming, the thieves.
I still haven't found lasting love.
I still want to hear viols
in the little beach hotel
that's torn down and gone.
I want to see again the fish
schooling and glittering like a veil
where the waves shove
against the breakwater. Gone
is the girl in her white slip
testing the chill with one bare foot.
It's too cold, but she goes in, so
carefully, oh.

Scrapbook

This is me, depressed out of my mind,
frailing the banjo, spilling red wine

on the white
king-sized

luckily hotel's and not my
goose down comforter, this is me

walking and waxing nostalgic through the girlish shadows
of tall palm trees, the *déjà vus*

flying through the scene
suddenly, like those three

unnameable and therefore beautiful white birds.
This is me as a slowly-tearing-itself-apart cloud

and marveling
at a fire palely and flamily

emerging from a fire bowl, wavering
up through little stones of cobalt glass. The air

wavers back. This is me in love
with the beauty of blue glass in flames, this is me on drugs

prescribed by my doctor
as I try once more

to sneak into the night's closely guarded city,
my hollow horse ready

to wreak my demons and Blue Morphos
on the citizens of my sleep. I am most

myself when flashing rapidly
my iridescent wings, drinking

the juice of fallen fruit. Then again
look for me under your bed

where the ugly premodern vampires
still hide. The undead and I are lying

in wait. We are very interested in you
though this is still me. We are unstable and true.

We believe in the one-ton rose
and the displaced toilet equally. Our blues

assume you understand
not much, and try to be alive, just as we do,

and that it may be helpful to hold the hand
of someone as lost as you.

Idioms for Rain

Wheelbarrows are falling in the Czech Republic
but in Wales, old ladies and sticks are landing
on the farms not yet carried off by owls,
knives and forks are clattering on the barns.
In the sky above New York City, one dark cloud
of dogs, one of feral cats, one of lawn gnomes
lined up with buckets, more clouds erupting
from their corncob pipes, the storm getting ready
to hammer the rooftop gardens and drive pigeons
into the arms of gargoyles. Gurgle. Gargle.
Some dragon is down with the flu, asking
who am I without my Kundalini breath, why
don't I have any friends, as soon as I'm better
I'm going to torch an elementary school.
In Union Square, the vendors are packing up
peaches and artisanal cheeses, castles
and pawns are being disappeared from
the chess players' tables, shitty art reinstalled
in the museums of panel vans.
Umbrellas and hoodies, tarps on the carts
of the homeless hunkering down
while leaves skid around. In Greece
chair legs drive themselves into stone
and sink into the Aegean, but in Syria
chemical weapons are descending
meaning raining down like secretaries
and restaurant workers from the towers,
meaning metaphor is being abandoned
for the hell of the real, meaning what falls
from the sky keeps falling. *Feallan*. Fission.
Thermonuclear but not yet cobalt.
What the rain said to the wind was not
You push and I'll pelt

but *Let's see who can destroy the most flowers*
though it also may have said *Sometimes*
I want to weep softly while you moan
over the seedlings. In Germany it rains
puppies where once rained Walther bullets,
and in Denmark, shoemakers' apprentices
land softly on the earth, and set off to teach
whom they can.

Plastic

A bunch of it is floating somewhere
way out in the Pacific.
If your love is deeper than the ocean,
then the surface of your love is a swirl
of swill, toothbrushes and swizzle sticks
carried by the inevitable current:
someone comes saying *oh oh shit baby baby*
then someone leaves the house key on the table
and sends a vaguely apologetic email.
Sunlight is bad for plastic. Imagine an Evian bottle
having a breakdown, getting eaten by a jellyfish
which is eaten by a bigger fish
which becomes a breaded, deep-fried rectangle
on a cafeteria tray. In an airport
you can eat with a metal fork
but the knife must be made of extruded polymers
to keep you from committing hara-kiri
as you return from delivering your lecture
on postmodern literary theory.
Back home, while you take your green canvas bag
to the store for beer and cereal,
the garbage in the ocean drifts, sidereal.
Think of the earth as a big snow globe
floating in space, only the snow is really sticky
and doesn't melt, even when the atmosphere
sizzles with migraine. Here come those zigzag lights
and a sickening feeling. Make that sinking.
Party cup, fake fruit, heart souvenir.
Even if your love is brighter than the sun,
the ick of snow keeps falling.
Everyone feels a little tender
when stabbed with a fork.

Here Be Dragons

I'm not done with the compass
& I'm still puzzling over the chart
all those squiggles and numbers
sea monsters prowling the depths
devouring ships serpent tusked whale
horsefish finned rhinoceros these
were my lovers these what dragged
me down what I wanted to be taken
to the underwater cities sirens
goatfish sphinxes whores I drank
in the taverns with pirates howler
monkeys my sea captain ancestors my
sozzled staggering fathers & returned
but not to any harbor only the curved
surface I sailed on

Divine

Oh hell, here's that dark wood again.
You thought you'd gotten through it –
middle of your life, the ogre turned into a mouse
and heart-stopped, the old hag almost done,
monsters hammered down
into their caves, werewolves outrun.
You'd come out of all that, into a field.
There was one man standing in it.
He held out his arms.
Ping went your iHeart
so you took off all your clothes.
Now there were two of you,
or maybe one, mashed back together
like sandwich halves,
oozing mayonnaise.
You lived on grapes and antidepressants
and the occasional small marinated mammal.
You watched the DVDs that dropped
from the DVD tree. Nothing
was forbidden you, so no worries there.
It rained a lot.
You planted some tomatoes.
Something bad had to happen
because no trouble, no story, so
Fuck you, fine, whatever,
here come more black trees
hung with sleeping bats
like ugly Christmas ornaments.
Don't you hate the holidays?
All that giving. All those wind-up
crèches, those fake silver icicles.
If you had a real one you could skewer
the big cursed heart of your undead love.

Instead you have a silver noodle
with which you must flay yourself.
Denial of pleasure,
death before death,
alone in the woods with a few bats
unfolding their creaky wings.

Seasonal Affective Disorder

Whoever came up with the acronym must have been happy
to think of everyone in winter walking around
saying 'I have SAD' instead of 'This time of year,
when the light leaves early and intimations of colder
hours settle over the houses like the great oppressive
oily scutes of a dragon's belly, I feel, I don't know,
a sense of ennui, a listlessness or lassitude
but more than that a definite undertow of dread
spreading over the waters of my already not-
exactly-sunny-to-begin-with-soul, if one can even
speak of the soul anymore, which is part of the problem,
isn't it, I mean, how do I even know if I have one,
given that I'm essentially a secular humanist and missing
whatever constellation or holy Smurf guides people
through their lives, Jesus or Mohammed and then
either Mohammed's son or second in command
depending on who you thought was the true
successor, which is only one of the problems still being
worked out by wars and car bombings just
as similar problems were solved in earlier times by flambéing
people in public after rack-induced confessions, and if
there's no immortal soul that's soon (too soon if you
ask me) to be either whirled up to heaven
like a cow shining in a tornado or else hauled screaming
into the underworld like a pig to a scalding tank,
that is, if we just, you know, stop, the filament worn out
or shooting through the glass and exploding the bulb
but either way, done, done for, pure nothing, the socket empty
for long enough to hear some prayers or poems and then
another little light bulb's screwed into place with
songs and lullabies and eventually loud music and drugs
which maybe I should be taking to overcome this thing
I hardly know how to describe, and which hardly anyone

wants to hear about since who can think too long
about such matters before all they want
is a drink or quiet place to curl up or TV to turn on
along with every light in the house,' and when your lover
(if you are lucky enough to have one even if you sometimes
feel bored and stifled by him/her or that maybe you could have
done better especially in terms of having more sex
money complex conversations a heavier plinth
for your nobly woeful statue) asks what's wrong
you can forget all this and simply say 'I have SAD'
since everyone knows that diagnosis is the first step
though on which stair or ladder is better left unmentioned
since they lead either way, but are best traveled
with someone steadying the rungs or waiting at the top
or bottom with a candle, a word, a cup of something hot
and not too bitter, that you can drink down, and proclaim
good.

Reel

The internist, the neurologist, the gastroenterologist –
Sinemat, Ritalin, Cerebrex –
the list written down and lost,
written again and taped to the wall and studied in bewilderment.

Bladder infections, anemia, dizziness, falls.
The husband dead, the house sold.
The trophies gone, and the people who saw the victories.

It sounds like the name of a creature concocted
from electricity and spare body parts,
jerked to ersatz life in a hail of blue sparks:

Dementia, darling! the scientist cries
before she fixes him with her burning eyes
and strangles him.

Postmodern Romance: Internet Dating

I'm tired of kissing nematodes,
splitting the check with scorpions,
listening to the spiritual autobiographies of slugs
over an infinitely repeated series
of banal gestural codes.
I'm thinking of dating trees next.
We could just stand around all night together.
We could stand each other.
I'd murmur, they'd rustle, the wind
would, like, do its wind thing,
without speaking. I hate speech.
Shut up shut up shut up I thought
as he flicked his tongue at the Peruvian tapas,
but the spell didn't work.
Get out of my inbox. I feel violated.
Not in a good way.
There's no one I want to inhale into my alveoli
like I did with you. There, I just made you
into a cigarette. If only
I could press your burning head
into the arrow wound, and twist you, slowly,
to cauterise it. Instead
I want another you, and then another.
You, in the morning after coffee.
Postprandial you. You, especially when I'm drinking.
But back to dating: I don't think I can.
If I read your profile online, I'd never write you.
But I miss all the sides of your face.
I miss the trees of your eyes.
I miss never licking the scar on your hand.
Last night I dreamed you came over
and stayed. If only I could buy

a little property in that dream
and not wake up sick
and freezing, endlessly hitting the return key.

Florida

And then there was the man who said, 'You look fatter
with your clothes off' and like a fool I didn't put them back on
but climbed into his bed beneath the little Tibetan prayer flags
and several images of Buddha haloed by a white light
I wished, at that moment, to dematerialise into,
especially when he asked me to get on top, but facing away from
      him,
so that I rose up and slid down looking at the knees and naked feet
of someone whom, an hour ago, I'd found attractive – in a way, I
      realised,
it was now a blessing not to have to look into his eyes, but still,
being fucked backwards while facing a stain on the wall that
      resembled Florida
was not quite the encounter I'd envisioned
standing in the bookstore that the Beats with their Blakean visions
and holy passionate excesses had made famous,
and my mind began to wander in order to avoid being present
for whatever was going on down there, eternally, it seemed,
and was that really his penis it felt like a speculum
as he groaned and I gazed at Florida thinking of orange groves
and all the nights in Pompano Beach my brothers and I played
      lighthouse tag,
dodging the beam that swept over the black sea and pale sand,
and of all the days I spent shirtless, climbing palm trees or
      squatting with a stick
over a washed-up blue translucent man o' war quivering in the wind
and of the time I dug a sand pit hoping to trap my crazy violent
      older brother,
anchoring the sharp swords of sticker plants upright in the bottom,
covering the hole with a blanket and just enough sand
and how was I going to lure him in there, maybe I could get him
      to chase me,
he was always chasing me, I could feel my anger

and the great happiness of impending revenge, imagining him
        falling in,
wishing I could cover him over and bury him forever,
while somewhere in the orange- scented light of a candle
in the universe behind me, my lover finished and I closed my eyes
and never, until now, turned around to look at him
sinking beneath the surface of the bed like a drowning sailor
thrown overboard from a great ship that centuries ago
rounded the cape and sailed on to another world.

Prosody Pathétique

Trochees tear your heart to tatters.
Lovers leave you broken, battered.
Fuck you, fuck off: spondees. So what.
Get high. Drop dead. Who cares. Life sucks.
Dactyls are you getting boozed in your underwear,
thinking of someone who used to be there.
These are iambs: *Dolor*. Despair.
And going on and on about your pain,
and sleeping pills, and dark and heavy rain.
Now for the anapests: in the end, you're alone.
In the bag, in the dark; in a terrible rut.
With a smirk, in a wink, the wolves tear you apart.

Darkening, Then Brightening

The sky keeps lying to the farmhouse,
lining up its heavy clouds
above the blue table umbrella,
then launching them over the river.
And the day feels hopeless
until it notices a few trees
dropping delicately their white petals
on the grass beside the birdhouse
perched on its wooden post,
the blinking fledglings stuffed inside
like clothes in a tiny suitcase. At first
you wandered lonely through the yard
and it was no help knowing Wordsworth
felt the same, but then Whitman
comforted you a little, and you saw
the grass as uncut hair, yearning
for the product to make it shine.
Now you lie on the couch beneath the skylight,
the sky starting to come clean,
mixing its cocktail of sadness and dazzle,
a deluge and then a digging out
and then enough time for one more
dance or kiss before it starts again,
darkening, then brightening.
You listen to the tall wooden clock
in the kitchen: its pendulum clicks
back and forth all day, and it chimes
with a pure sound, every hour on the hour,
though it always mistakes the hour.

Pareidolia

(perception of pattern and meaning from natural randomness)

The skillet burns that appeared on the tortilla
rolled by Maria Rubio in 1977
looked just like the face of Jesus.
In the bathtub this morning,
a few strands of my hair
formed a wavery peace symbol.
Would you pay to see this miracle?
What about snowflakes –
the cloud they fall from this afternoon
resembles another cloud
which resembles a tennis ball
served by my dead mother in 1947.
Surely that proves that all life on earth
is in a big intergalactic bath towel woven.
Somewhere a snowflake pukes on its shoes
in a convenience store parking lot.
At Jiggles, a half-naked snowflake
pole-dances in panties on the bar.
Across the world, another little snowflake
blows itself up in a crowded café.
Snow everywhere descending.
It gathers to a whiteness.
Why don't we lie down together,
wing-bones touching?
You look like someone I used to love,
only colder.

Party

I know we've just met and everything
but I'd really like to fall apart on you now.
I'd like to think you're the kind of person
who'd refill my glass all night, then pour me
shitfaced into your car and take me home with you
so I could regurgitate salmon and triple cream brie
and chocolate strawberries into your toilet,
and then you'd cook me a little something –
I'd like to think you're the kind of person who cooks –
while I rambled incoherently about my loneliness.
I know we've just met but I feel like maybe
you'd feed me and tuck me into your big bed
and only touch me as you covered me with the comforter.
I feel like you own a comforter. I also somehow sense
that your family was extremely dysfunctional
in a way that differs from mine only in surface details,
like which person was the black hole
and which the distant, faint mark in space
that might have been a star. I feel all that.
I feel kind of, I don't know, like my inner space heater
and TV and washing machine are all going at once.
Do you own a coffee grinder?
I have an ice cube tray. The last ice disappeared
a few months ago, into the freezer mist.
I miss that ice but once the mist gets hold of it,
it's gone for good. Unrelenting mist. Many-headed
mist. Who knew mist had undone so many.
I feel like my underwear would fit in your silverware caddy.
It's just a feeling, though. I could be wrong about that.
Could you get me another drink now?
I think we have chemistry. I really need a lab partner.
Could I just, you know, let my molecules separate
while you keep an eye on the burner? The flame's kind of fickle.
Here's hoping it doesn't go out.

Elegy for Jon

The lighthouse beam sweeps over me.
I never trusted the sea, always shoving
into coves, scattering salt-glyphs
over tourists hotels, smashing
trawlers and rowboats to sticks. I keep
finding myself beside it, wishing
it would turn into a lake
with maybe a dock floating close to shore.
If not a lake, then a river
between canyons. If not a river
then a big moonlit piano
stocked with fish. *Play irretrievably*
with the lid closed,
Satie wrote on one of his scores
but I never discovered which one
or how the music sounded
but this is one way it might go
on a beach where ugly kelp
and a yellowed piano key are flung
from the waves. I wish the earth
had waited a little longer
before swallowing my brother.
I wish the sea would stop
swallowing his name while it goes on
kissing the sand, laying
another cold wreath at my feet.

White Flower, Red Flower

He spent a year playing Death in *La Traviata*,
ruining a camellia in the first act
and smoking a Gauloise in the last
while Violetta succumbed.
Here in the former monastery
the monks succumbed, giving way
to the four of us drinking Sagrantino
and telling stories in the gravel courtyard
under the pasta-shaped stars.
Out in the olive orchard, a mouse
succumbs to a screech owl
and down the hillside, the old painter
who owns this place is yielding,
slowly, to cancer, but today
she recited Montale's poem –
the sunflower crazed with light –
and today we saw the white dog
whose job it is to guide a few sheep
out of Chagall's canvases into the lushness
of the present moment. That moment
has already succumbed to the next
but here we still are, sitting at a small
round table in the dark, drinking
darkness from our glasses,
growing dizzy with darkness,
past midnight now, the date turned over,
date of my friend's birth so more darkness
is poured. In the *chiesa* is a painting
of Jesus emerging from his tomb,
hatted like a Veneto farmer.
In our room is a red-robed Virgin, tiny adult Savior
on her lap. A cracked and mottled mirror
on the marble-topped wood bureau,

sepia family portraits on the walls.
Gran Dio, morir si giovane,
sang Pavarotti and Sutherland,
Alfredo and Violetta, she with surprising brio
for someone about to droop, dead,
into her lover's arms. But what difference
your age; everyone's here until
they're not, gone but in some weird
way still hovering in the air,
in a cracked mirror, in the eyes
of those grandparents and great-aunts.
Enter from stage left the red
shock of wings, a disturbance in the trees
easily mistaken for wind.

Sleep Stage

In the dream, my mother could again
get out of bed, but only to stand

before a black mirror, so really
not a good dream after all,

and not prescient since the next day
there she still was, bed cranked up,

no teeth, so a kind of swallow hole where
her lips used to be. Into the hole

I maneuvered a spoon of green mush
but then skipped that and the squash

to give her all the pudding,
and went sneaking

to the bathroom to dump the remains
so the nurse wouldn't know. Dreams,

what are they, anyway: collage art,
trash bins, intergalactic interfaces,

maybe random missile fire
from oppressed realities. The blockade

creates a black market, tunnels are dug
to smuggle goats and weapons.

Dead father laughing at a party.
Ex-lover saving the plane

from crashing into the ice-locked river.
Last night there were lions everywhere

except inside the circle I drew around myself
with a stick in the dirt.

I got into bed with her.
Soon she'll be scattered, probably

over a tennis court somewhere,
which sounds like a dream but won't be.

Dream the Night My Brother Dies

Whichever way I turn there is a door.
I run in and out of the doors.
In one room, inconsolable weeping.
In another, a sad animal regards me.
In a third, a hole in the floor.
I lower my bucket
a long way down on its white rope.

Candy Heart Valentine

In the story of the three little words, things turn out badly:
one is washed overboard, another ends trapped under a machine
drinking and dialing, the third is still apologising to some rocks.
I've forgotten how to swim, and the sharks are circling. Love
is hopeless in exactly zero of the Hollywood movies I've watched, alone
in bed or else sitting in the overbuttered dark,
someone's hand on my thigh, my hand on someone's stirring
private parts. You were someone to me once, but now I've razored
through most of the frames. I only occasionally hear the clatter
and dying fall before the projector stops. Love, according to the Greeks,
came in four flavors, *eros* being the most likely to turn to old gum
and so end up smashed on a sidewalk by the boots
and spiked heels of happier passersby, flattened under the swivel
of stroller wheels. You know what I miss? I miss lying next to you
feeling like a lifeboat roped to an ocean liner. Love isn't love,
according to Shakespeare, if it's confused about whether it's a star
or distant satellite, if it's a wine stain that succumbs
to a little seltzer water. You know what else I miss: when you strummed
your electric lyre, your plectrum flashing in bar light. I still see
a pink cloud where the spill was. Love is deeper than nothing.
You're not here. I'm writing our story in small block letters. LOVE
machine-mixed, stamped into dough. YOU. You know. You know.

Last Lights

People are still having children it's unbelievable
tucking them into strollers and car seats still
washing their mouths out with soap maybe the way
ours were washed but never got clean because we're still
filthy with grief and longing and the knowledge
that the earth is a great spheroid head
with an oblate headache that hurricane swirl that
skull crack running through it still meeting for drinks
to talk about movies and exes still having sex
for the first time like horses on the Discovery channel a nuzzle
for foreplay then he mounts her then gallops off
still galloping still coming to the fence for an apple
engineered for redness for texture still bleeding
in the street for a whistle a word a sweetness rises
from the earth anyway still writing poems without
the grandeur of anything just a girl on the corner
with a rescued pigeon on her shoulder and two
little dogs one with its tongue permanently flagging out
the other turning mad circles but the pigeon
gently pecking at her lower lip in gratitude and love.

Name That Means Holy in Greek

(for Aya)

Today I heard your name shouted
by a short-order cook
flipping scallion pancakes in a grease-
grimed Chinese restaurant.
He said it meant *Wow*
which is the best word I know
for the unutterable sublime. *Wow*
is how I had the dumb luck
to become your young and terrified mother
not knowing how to hold you
in the hospital parking lot
while your father got the car.
It seemed to take a long time.
Wow, it seemed to take ten minutes
for you to get your driver's license
and move away to New York.
I remember the moment we made you
and knew we had, your father
lifting himself up off the bed and laughing.
Little hawk, Sumerian goddess,
Kachina that races the wind.
The verses of the Quran are Ayas.
In Japanese, full of color, or beauty,
though once inked for me
as 'Tomorrow's arrow'. The secret
ingredient in the chef's special, a marinade
containing Aya. First word
spoken by a rose, last word the trees
say at night as they lie down
in the forests and fields, last sound
I'll make, if I can still speak at the end,
my palindrome, sword, storm wind.

The Givens

Someone will bump into you and not apologise, someone will wear
the wrong dress to the party, another lurch drunk into the table
of cheeses and pastries at the memorial service, someone will tell you
she's sorry it's out of her hands as though everything isn't already.
One day the toilet will mysteriously detach its little chain
from its rubber thingie and refuse to flush, in the throes
of whatever existential crisis toilets experience after so much human
waste, so many tampons it wasn't supposed to swallow, so many pills
washed down because someone in a fit of sobriety tossed them in,
    though later
regretted it but too late, they're gone, someone kneeling to empty
a meal, a bottle of wine, too many mango–cucumber–vodka cocktails made
from a recipe by Martha Stewart. Someone will have seen Martha
    Stewart
in a restaurant, surrounded by admirers; criminals
will order quail, world leaders stab their forks into small countries
to hold them still for their serrated knives. Ben Franklin said
nothing is certain but death and taxes and he was wrong
about the taxes but then again, right about the impermanency
of the Constitution. No one will come to your door to give you a stack
of bills imprinted with Ben Franklin's face, but a Jehovah's Witness
will find you one day to tell you there is no Hell and that the souls
of the wicked will be annihilated. Someone will love you but not enough,
someone else send gift-wrapped pheromones to your vomeronasal organ,
which will promptly destroy them like bugs in a zapper. These are but
    a few
of the many givens, and it's tempting to boil them down to just two
like Franklin did but I prefer Duchamp's '_Étant donnés_', – 1. The
    Waterfall,
2. The Illuminating Gas, water and light, as it was when God began
to pronounce those words in his marble bathroom but given how it's all
gone since then he probably should have skipped the part where clay
sits up and rubs its eyes, looking for something to fuck or kill.

The rain, the lightning. The river town, the fireworks off the dock.

Someone will run through a lawn sprinkler, someone else open a
      hydrant.

Someone will pull you from the fire, someone else wrap you in flames.

Invisible Signals

I like it when I forget about time with its cleaning rag
and the drunken gods standing ready with their fly swatters
while I hide in the curtains. I like thinking about the friends I miss,
one with her twenty-four hour sobriety chip,
one making pozole while her dog
frets in its cage in the kitchen, one helping her sister drag
the oxygen tank to the bathroom. One is preparing her lecture
on the present moment, not mentioning me but here I am,
or was, watching this slut of a river smear kisses all over
east Manhattan, letting the ferries slide under her dress,
her face lit up and flushed. I like to think of my friends
imagining me so we're all together in one big mental cloud
passing between the river and outer space. Here we are
not dissolving but dropping our shadows like darkening
handkerchiefs on the water. One crying by a lake,
one rehabbing her knee for further surgery. One
pulling a beer from the fridge, holding it, deciding.
One calling the funeral home, then taking up
the guitar, the first tentative chord floating out,
hanging suspended in the air.

FROM

The Philosopher's Club

(1994)

What the Dead Fear

On winter nights, the dead
see their photographs slipped
from the windows of wallets,
their letters stuffed in a box
with the clothes for Goodwill.
No one remembers their jokes,
their nervous habits, their dread
of enclosed places.
In these nightmares, the dead feel
the soft nub of the eraser
lightening their bones. They wake up
in a panic, go for a glass of milk
and see the moon, the fresh snow,
the stripped trees.
Maybe they fix a turkey sandwich,
or watch the patterns on the TV.
It's all a dream anyway.
In a few months
they'll turn the clocks ahead,
and when they sleep they'll know the living
are grieving for them, unbearably lonely
and indifferent to beauty. On these nights
the dead feel better. They rise
in the morning, refreshed, and when the cut
flowers are laid before their names
they smile like shy brides. Thank you,
thank you, they say. You shouldn't have,
they say, but very softly, so it sounds
like the wind, like nothing human.

China Camp, CA

Here's the long trough, covered by a screen,
where they cleaned shrimp.
Easier to imagine their catch
than to glimpse the ghosts of the fishermen
who lived here in these few wood buildings,
some now in need of repair, tin-roofed,
boarded windows whose gaps we peer through
to see shadowed dirt, a rusted wheelbarrow.
Of their boats, only a lone hull remains,
hauled to the sand and half-sunk there,
surrounded by chain link.
Yet everything is the same: the bay,
tamed by the curve of land that makes the cove,
still curls in
easily as hands turning over
to close, and close again, a book whose pages
ceaselessly open. Shards of their dishes
and rice bowls wash back
with the frail skeletons of crabs, glass
dulled and polished, indecipherable bits
of broken shells, jade-green kelp.
It's said they were driven out by hatred,
or concern that they'd leave nothing
for the next boats, but no one recorded
where they went. This was the home they made,
miles from China: brief shore,
a sky brushed with clouds,
gulls following them in each sunset,
the women stirring soup
with buried spoons, lost silk
of their sashes, black hair unpinned
and carried out with the tide,
tangling in the empty nets and sinking
to the coldest dark water.

The Concept of God

Years later, nothing inside the church
has changed. Not the dusty light,
not the white feet of the statues
or the boys in their pale smocks kneeling before the candles.
Not the cool basement, the paper plates of donuts
set out by the coffee urns.
Not the bathroom with its stall doors open
on a row of immaculate toilets,
blue water in the bowls,
a small wrapped soap on each sink.
Forever the two girls leaning against the wall
in the deep quiet, sharing a lipsticked Salem
and watching themselves in the mirror,
forever the priest nodding in the confessional,
opening and closing his small window.
Always my father moving down the rows
of bored, sonorous voices, passing the long-handled basket,
my mother with his handkerchief pinned over her hair.
Always, too, his coffin before the altar, my brother
stammering a eulogy, the long line of parked cars
spattered with snow. Always this brief moment
when the candles shudder, then resume,
and the girl holding the cigarette peers more closely
into the mirror, startled for an instant
at how old, how much like a woman
it makes her look.

Full Moon

All over the city
something gets into people.
Women tucking in their kids
close their eyes,
think of men they should have followed off buses.
Girls rouge their cheeks with lipstick,
their bodies telling lies
to anyone who'll listen.
Cars with their lights off glide
under the trees, headed for the ocean.
The men going through garbage cans
rifle Burger King bags for a few
pale fries. They lie down
in doorways. In dreams
their mothers check their foreheads for fever.
Refugees sit up
studying old photographs they enter
like water, going under.
Moon, take them down.
Desire is a cold drink
that scalds the heart.
Somewhere women are standing
at their windows, like lit candles,
and boys in Army boots
go dancing through the streets,
singing, and shoot
at anything that moves.

The Call

A man opens a magazine,
women with no clothes,
their eyes blacked out.
He dials a number,
hums a commercial
under his breath. A voice
tells him he can do
anything he wants to her.
He imagines standing her
against a wall, her saying
Oh baby you feel so good.
It's late. The woman
on the phone yawns,
trails the cord to the hall
to look in on her daughter.
She's curled with one
leg off the couch.
The woman shoulders the receiver,
tucks a sheet and whispers
Yes. Do it. Yes.
She goes to the kitchen,
opens another Diet Pepsi, wonders
how long it will take him and where
she can find a cheap winter coat.
Remembering the bills
she flips off the light.
He's still saying *Soon*,
turning his wheelchair right,
left, right. A tube runs down
his pants leg. Sometimes
he thinks he feels something,
stops talking to concentrate
on movement down there.

Hello, the woman says.
You still on?
She rubs a hand over her eyes.
Blue shadow comes off on her fingers.
Over the faint high hiss
of the open line
she hears the wheels knock
from table to wall.
What's that, she says.
Nothing, he tells her,
and they both
listen to it.

The Philosopher's Club

After class Thursday nights
the students meet at the Philosopher's Club.
It's right around the corner from the streetcar tracks
at the West Portal tunnel. No one bothers
to check IDs. Five or six of them
get shooters and talk – about sex, usually.
Let me tell you about this dildo I bought,
one girl says. She describes how it looks
when all the gadgets attached to it are going at once.
My girlfriend is pregnant, says one of the boys.
That's nothing, says another, I've got twins
I've never seen. It goes on like this all semester.
Gradually they learn each other's stories:
the girl raped at knifepoint in Florida,
the kid whose old man shot seven people
in a trailer park outside Detroit.
Life is weird, they agree, touching glasses.
The bartender flips channels on the TV,
the sound turned down.
Spoiled brats, he thinks. He imagines a woman
with the blonde's legs, the brunette's tits.
Dynasty looks boring and he quits
at a black-and-white newsreel about the Nazi camps –
piles of heads with their mouths open,
bodies with arms like chicken wings. On the jukebox
Otis Redding sings 'Try a Little Tenderness'.
One of the regulars stands there
popping his gum, jamming in selections.
The students, smashed, are hugging each other.
I love you, they all say. Outside, in the rain,
people are boarding a lit streetcar.

As it jolts towards the tunnel
some of them look back at the bar,
its staticky neon sign
the last thing they see as they enter the dark.

The Last Poem About the Dead

sounds like this: a long sweet silence
the next soul breaks as it drops,
the way a fish flops back
slapping the quiet water,
the next slippery, gleaming body
that's still, this minute, alive:
my mother, the brothers I love
but can't get close to,
or my daughter,
please God not my daughter,
not her made-up songs
as she moves her dolls from kitchen to bed
in the small house, take
anyone else, my lover with his warm sex
pressed against me,
brush him off of me like a winged insect,
I don't care what you do with him,
you can have all of them,
my family, my best friend,
take them, but not my girl.
And if it's me
then the silence doesn't stop
when I hit the water, thrashing,
it goes on unless you do it
for me, make the poem I'd make
drifting down to them
without voice; oh, tell me
how to tell you what it's like.

The Sound

Marc says the suffering that we don't see
still makes a sort of sound – a subtle, soft
noise, nothing like the cries or screams that we
might think of – more the slight scrape of a hat doffed
by a quiet man, ignored as he stands back
to let a lovely woman pass, her dress
just brushing his coat. Or else it's like a crack
in an old foundation, slowly widening, the stress
and slippage going on unnoticed by
the family upstairs, the daughter leaving
for a date, her mother's resigned sigh
when she sees her. It's like the heaving
of a stone into a lake, before it drops.
It's shy, it's barely there. It never stops.

First Poem For You

I love to touch your tattoos in complete
darkness, when I can't see them. I'm sure of
where they are, know by heart the neat
lines of lightning pulsing just above
your nipple, can find, as if by instinct, the blue
swirls of water on your shoulder where a serpent
twists, facing a dragon. When I pull you
to me, taking you until we're spent
and quiet on the sheets, I love to kiss
the pictures in your skin. They'll last until
you're seared to ashes; whatever persists
or turns to pain between us, they will still
be there. Such permanence is terrifying.
So I touch them in the dark; but touch them, trying.

Them

That summer they had cars, soft roofs crumpling
over the back seats. Soft, too, the delicate fuzz
on their upper lips and the napes of their necks,
their uneven breath, their tongues tasting
of toothpaste. We stole the liquor
glowing in our parents' cabinets, poured it
over the cool cubes of ice with their hollows
at each end, as though a thumb had pressed
into them. The boys rose, dripping, from long
blue pools, the water slick on their backs
and bellies, a sugary glaze; they sat easily on high
lifeguard chairs, eyes hidden by shades,
or came up behind us to grab the fat we hated
around our waists. For us it was the chaos
of makeup on a bureau, the clothes we tried on
and on, the bras they unhooked, pushed
up, and when they moved their hard
hidden cocks against us we were always
princesses, our legs locked. By then we knew
they would come, climb the tower, slay anything
to get to us. We knew we had what they wanted:
the breasts, the thighs, the damp hairs pressed flat
under our panties. All they asked was that we let them
take it. They would draw it out of us like
sticky taffy, thinner and thinner until it snapped
and they had it. And we would grow up
with that lack, until we learned how to
name it, how to look in their eyes and see nothing
we had not given them; and we could still
have it, we could reach right down into their
bodies and steal it back.

Gravity

Carrying my daughter to bed
I remember how light she once was,
no more than a husk in my arms.
There was a time I could not put her down,
so frantic was her crying if I tried
to pry her from me, so I held her
for hours at night, walking up and down the hall,
willing her to fall asleep. She'd grow quiet,
pressed against me, her small being alert
to each sound, the tension in my arms, she'd take
my nipple and gaze up at me,
blinking back fatigue she'd fight whatever terror
waited beyond my body in her dark crib. Now
that she's so heavy I stagger beneath her,
she slips easily from me, down
into her own dreaming. I stand over her bed,
fixed there like a second, dimmer star,
though the stars are not fixed: someone
once carried the weight of my life.

Beds

All night I turn between
lover and daughter, holding one
and then the other. Before dawn
I have slipped out of bed,
leaving them together,
the man's broad chest uncovered,
the child's blonde hair
hiding her face.
I remember nights as a child,
wedged between my parents,
the sinking down to sleep surrounded
by familiar things. When death
beats its wings at the window
I hope I am not standing
alone in the kitchen
with a cup and a hairbrush,
watching doves on a wire.
I want to curl up
in that dim, disordered bed
where all my loves lie,
elbow to cheek;
I want the brief reprieve
as the angel who came for me
pauses, uncertain,
trying to distinguish one breath
from another.

Tell Me

(2000)

The Numbers

How many nights have I lain here like this, feverish with plans,
with fears, with the last sentence someone spoke, still trying to finish
a conversation already over? How many nights were wasted
in not sleeping, how many in sleep – I don't know
how many hungers there are, how much radiance or salt, how many
    times
the world breaks apart, disintegrates to nothing and starts up again
in the course of an ordinary hour. I don't know how God can bear
seeing everything at once: the falling bodies, the monuments and
    burnings,
the lovers pacing the floors of how many locked hearts. I want to
    close
my eyes and find a quiet field in fog, a few sheep moving toward a
    fence.
I want to count them, I want them to end. I don't want to wonder
how many people are sitting in restaurants about to close down,
which of them will wander the sidewalks all night
while the pies revolve in the refrigerated dark. How many days
are left of my life, how much does it matter if I manage to say
one true thing about it – how often have I tried, how often
failed and fallen into depression? The field is wet, each grassblade
gleaming with its own particularity, even here, so that I can't help
asking again, the white sky filling with footprints, bricks,
with mutterings over rosaries, with hands that pass over flames
before covering the eyes. I'm tired, I want to rest now.
I want to kiss the body of my lover, the one mouth, the simple name
without a shadow. Let me go. How many prayers
are there tonight, how many of us must stay awake and listen?

Glass

In every bar there's someone sitting alone and absolutely absorbed
by whatever he's seeing in the glass in front of him,
a glass that looks ordinary, with something clear or dark
inside it, something partially drunk but never completely gone.
Everything's there: all the plans that came to nothing,
the stupid love affairs, and the terrifying ones, the ones where actual
    happiness
opened like a hole beneath his feet and he fell in, then lay helpless
while the dirt rained down a little at a time to bury him.
And his friends are there, cracking open six-packs, raising the bottles,
the click of their meeting like the sound of a pool cue
nicking a ball, the wrong ball, that now edges, black and shining,
toward the waiting pocket. But it stops short, and at the bar the lone
    drinker
signals for another. Now the relatives are floating up
with their failures, with cancer, with plateloads of guilt
and a little laughter, too, and even beauty – some afternoon from
    childhood,
a lake, a ball game, a book of stories, a few flurries of snow
that thicken and gradually cover the earth until the whole
world's gone white and quiet, until there's hardly a world
at all, no traffic, no money or butchery or sex,
just a blessed peace that seems final but isn't. And finally
the glass that contains and spills this stuff continually
while the drinker hunches before it, while the bartender gathers
up empties, gives back the drinker's own face. Who knows what it
    looks like;
who cares whether or not it was young once, or ever lovely,
who gives a shit about some drunk rising to stagger toward
the bathroom, some man or woman or even lost
angel who recklessly threw it all over – heaven, the ether,
the celestial works – and said, *Fuck it, I want to be human?*
Who believes in angels, anyway? Who has time for anything

but their own pleasures and sorrows, for the few good people
they've managed to gather around them against the uncertainty,
against afternoons of sitting alone in some bar
with a name like the Embers or the Ninth Inning or the Wishing
	Well?
Forget that loser. Just tell me who's buying, who's paying;
Christ but I'm thirsty, and I want to tell you something,
come close I want to whisper it, to pour
the words burning into you, the same words for each one of you,
listen, it's simple, I'm saying it now, while I'm still sober,
while I'm not about to weep bitterly into my own glass,
while you're still here – don't go yet, stay, stay,
give me your shoulder to lean against, steady me, don't let me drop,
I'm so in love with you I can't stand up.

Quantum

You know how hard it is sometimes just to walk on the streets
   downtown, how everything enters you
the way the scientists describe it – photons streaming through
   bodies, caroming off the air, the impenetrable brick
of buildings an illusion – sometimes you can feel how porous you
   are, how permeable, and the man lurching in circles
on the sidewalk, cutting the space around him with a tin can and
   saying *Uhh! Uhhhh! Uhh!* over and over
is part of it, and the one in gold chains leaning against the glass
   of the luggage store is, and the one who steps toward you
from his doorway, meaning to ask something apparently simple,
   like *What's the time*, something you know
you can no longer answer; he's part of it, the body of the world
   which is also yours and which keeps insisting
you recognise it. And the trouble is, you do, but it's happening
   here, among the crowds and exhaust smells,
and you taste every greasy scrap of paper, the globbed spit you
   step over, your tongue is as thick with dirt
as though you've fallen on your hands and knees to lick the oil-
   scummed street, as sour as if you've been drinking
the piss of those men passing their bottle in the little park with its
   cement benches and broken fountain. And it's no better
when you descend the steps to the Metro and some girl's wailing
   off-key about her heart – your heart –
over the awful buzzing of the strings, and you hurry through the
   turnstile, fumbling out the money that's passed
from how many hands into yours, getting rid of all your change
   except one quarter you're sure she sees
lying blind in your pocket as you get into a car and the doors seal
   themselves behind you. But still it isn't over.
Because later, when you're home, looking out your window at the
   ocean, at the calm of the horizon line,

and the apple in your hand glows in that golden light that
      happens in the afternoon, suffusing you with something
you're sure is close to peace, you think of the boy bagging
      groceries at Safeway, of how his face was flattened
in a way that was familiar – bootheel of a botched chromosome –
      and you remember his canceled blue eyes,
and his hands, flaking, rash-reddened, that lifted each thing and
      caressed it before placing it carefully
in your sack, and the monotonous song he muttered, *paper or plastic,*
      paper or plastic, his mouth slack,
a teardrop of drool at the corner; and you know he's a part of it
      too, raising the fruit to your lips you look out
at the immense and meaningless blue and know you're inside it,
      you realise you're eating him now.

Theodicy

Suppose we could see evil with such clarity we wouldn't hesitate
to stamp it out like stray sparks from a fire. Look at those boys
shooting baskets in the park, jostling each other to hook the ball
through the iron circle at the end of the asphalt – what if you knew

a secret about one of them? Shirtless, he stands vibrating
at the edge of an imaginary line, the orange globe trembling
at the tips of his fingers, sweat drawing the light into his skin –
what if he'd done something unspeakable, something I can't

talk about but know you can imagine, to the one
you love most in this world? Your child, maybe,
or the person whose body you know so well you can see it
simply by closing your eyes – What if he'd broken that body;

do you think if I handed you a gun you would walk up
to that shining boy and use it? You might think first
that maybe he couldn't help himself, maybe he was trying
as he stood there concentrating on his shot to stop the noise

of some relentless machine grinding away in his brain,
the same one you hear in yours sometimes, bearing down until
you can't tell what's true anymore, or good. Suppose God
began to have that trouble. Suppose the first man

turned out cruel and stupid, a cartoon creature
that farted and giggled continuously; suppose the woman ripped
saplings from the earth all day and refused to speak
or be grateful for anything. What if they decided to torment

the smaller, weaker beasts, and just as God was about
to strike them dead and start over they turned toward each other
and discovered fucking, and the serpent whispered *Look at them*
and God's head filled with music while the wild sparks leaped

from their bodies, bright as the new stars in the heavens.

Garbage

Don't think about where it goes
after you tie it up in its white bag and squash it down
into the can dragged out to the curb. Don't think
of the stink of the truck backing up, or the men in their filthy gloves
hanging off the sides, cursing in the near-dark of a new day
in which, somewhere, someone is about to be thrown into a cell
the way garbage is thrown into a deep pit for burning,
the way bodies are thrown in to be shoveled over.
Don't think about the dump, the scavenging rats,
the reeking piles they tunnel through – the flattened shoes,
the dolls with their eyes torn out, the pennies, the lost
wedding ring, whatever's found its way there and won't return
except as a stain, a bad smell on the air, a poison
seeding the clouds until it rains back down. But today
the weather's lovely; look at the sky, its purity,
its nullity, only gulls crossing it on their way
to the beaches. Don't let the gulls remind you
of how they dive beak-first into fish, of fish floating up with the
      sewage.
Especially don't think of dead things, or of vultures, how they wait
      so patiently
while something is bleeding into the dirt, and then jostle each other
as they hunch black-frocked around it, feeding the way everyone feeds;
oh, don't think now of all the food you've wasted,
scraped off plates or gone bad on the shelf, in the fridge,
you couldn't help it, you meant to save everyone, the children
      especially,
but it keeps filling up the house: the thick black print of newspapers,
the petitions for money with lists of their names, their actual faces,
they're still alive, they're out there with the guards
and the soldiers and the flies, so don't think of how clean
your house is, don't think for a minute you've gotten it all,
look at your hands, they're covered with it, you can try

70

to wash them or else plunge them in; even one finger, take it and
     scrape
up a little of the sludge and the muck and the stench
of the human, feel how the barest hope clings there.

Things That Don't Happen

Is there a place they go – the gold stalks, the umbels, the new shoots,
when the seeds rot in the fields or are eaten by birds? Is there a city
    someone meant to build
where your car is humming steadily through the streets, while here
    the ignition
turns over with a dull sound announcing silence, and you trudge
    back to the house,
the appointment canceled, erased from the date book, and a different
    day starts, the way
it starts for someone in a farmhouse kitchen, with a mother who's
    suddenly
a widow, an uncle who says *Don't let any niggers touch him* so that for
    a moment
the black coroner lays out the body, and gently closes the eyes
while the wife slips on her old nightgown and the son whispers on
    the phone
to his lover, and the monsignor prepares his eulogy –
this is a eulogy for the things that don't happen, for the stillborn,
the unstamped passport, the ring given back or pawned, or simply
    tossed
into a drawer with the final papers, the ones that say you failed
as everything fails, while each day the tiny accumulations, the
    insignificant actions,
destroy those shimmerings in the air, those sparks thrown off, the fire
    of the actual
consuming everything. The ice settles in the empty glass beside my
    bed, a sudden,
startling *click*, a latch, an opening or closing, I can't tell which; I
    could get up, pour
another shot, stop trying to explain how it obsesses me, each day
the *not* of what is: this lover's mouth and not the last one's, this
    dream
that isn't premonition and vanishes on waking, incoherency refusing

to coalesce, the words stoppered in a bottle that floats to the
   horizon's edge
and goes down, flaring for an instant. And each day the terror, your
   house
with its blood-smirched doorpost, the angel passing over but stopping
   somewhere else:
brains sprayed on a brick wall or leaking into the dirt, bodies in the
   river carried down
with the current, river where one fish feels a hook tearing through
   its gills and rises
frantically into the air. But why should we be sad; shouldn't we be
   breaking out
the champagne, thinking of the would-be suicide sweating in a room,
   the pistol
with its rusted firing-pin flung onto the bed, all the black shoes safe
   in the back
of the closet; and of the boy in Birkenau, his death that doesn't
   happen
so that two generations later, in Brooklyn, a girl can kneel down
to place a small stone on his stone, and stand to brush the dirt off
   her knees?
Isn't the loss held in abeyance each day, the benign tumor, the
   wreckage
at the intersection where you might have been standing, except that
   you caught the streetcar;
but really there is no streetcar, none of this is happening – it's trying
   to but I can't help
realising how hopeless it is: as fast as I have you step up, pay the fare,
struggle into a seat with your packages, I've kept you from a thousand
   better things.
I should let you lie in bed late at night, awake but not alone; I should
   nestle you
against the one true lover you haven't let yourself long for in years
but who is finally here, who's not ever leaving. I should seal you up
with the breast, the kiss. Nightingale, nipple, tongue dipping into
   the real,

the taste of it, the singing, the virtual lark, the light beginning but not
    yet
day, not clothes yet, not shame or betrayal, just the lovers too unironic
    to survive
anywhere but here. So this is the end, because I want to keep my
    stupid faith
in romance, in the idea of love, and if you would just let it go on
    forever this way
you wouldn't have to go out into the nothing where something is
    waiting
especially for you, though what it is I can't tell you, only that it begins
as soon as you stop listening, and turn away, only that it happens now.

Night of the Living, Night of the Dead

When the dead rise in movies they're hideous
and slow. They stagger uphill toward the farmhouse
like drunks headed home from the bar.
Maybe they only want to lie down inside
while some room spins around them, maybe that's why
they bang on the windows while the living
hammer up boards and count out shotgun shells.
The living have plans: to get to the pickup parked
in the yard, to drive like hell to the next town.
The dead with their leaky brains,
their dangling limbs and ruptured hearts,
are sick of all that. They'd rather stumble
blind through the field until they collide
with a tree, or fall through a doorway
like they're the door itself, sprung from its hinges
and slammed flat on the linoleum. That's the life
for a dead person: *wham, wham, wham*
until you forget your name, your own stinking
face, the reason you jolted awake
in the first place. Why are you here,
whatever were you hoping as you lay
in your casket like a dumb clarinet?
You know better now. The soundtrack's depressing
and the living hate your guts. Come closer
and they'll show you how much. *Wham, wham, wham,*
you're killed again. Thank God this time
they're burning your body, thank God
it can't drag you around any more
except in nightmares, late-night reruns
where you lift up the lid, and crawl out
once more, and start up the hill toward the house.

Virgin Spring

It's a terrible scene, the two men talking to the girl who foolishly
    lets them lead her away
from the road she's taking to church, the men raping and killing
    her, the young boy with them
watching, then left for a while with her body. But the film's next
    scene is more terrible
in some ways, the men and boy arriving at the house where the
    girl's parents live, but not
knowing, and the parents not knowing, either, offering a meal, all
    of them sitting together, breaking bread
at a long table – Is that the most awful, or is it when one man
    tries to sell the mother
her murdered daughter's clothes? – and she takes them,
    pretending to consider. Though how
could she pretend at that moment, how control herself? Yet she
    does; she goes outside,
locking them in the barn, and runs to her husband, to whom the
    task of killing them falls.
So it goes on – rape, betrayal, murder, not even the boy is spared.
    And what about the father,
swearing to build a church on the spot his daughter was killed,
    and the miracle of the water
gushing forth from the ground when they lift her body – Is that
    enough, is there some sort
of balance now, good following evil, revenge annulled, the family
    cleansed? What about
the other, dark-haired sister, the pregnant one, who had been a
    few yards behind on the road
to church that morning, who had followed the men and watched
    from a safe distance
while they erased the girl, her prettiness, her spoiled ways, her
    stupid innocence –

I don't know what to make of the sister. She's the one who knows
    the world is brutal
and goes on, scattering seed for the hogs, the one who says
    nothing, the one who survives.

New Year's Day

The rain this morning falls
on the last of the snow

and will wash it away. I can smell
the grass again, and the torn leaves

being eased down into the mud.
The few loves I've been allowed

to keep are still sleeping
on the West Coast. Here in Virginia

I walk across the fields with only
a few young cows for company.

Big-boned and shy,
they are like girls I remember

from junior high, who never
spoke, who kept their heads

lowered and their arms crossed against
their new breasts. Those girls

are nearly forty now. Like me,
they must sometimes stand

at a window late at night, looking out
on a silent backyard, at one

rusting lawn chair and the sheer walls
of other people's houses.

They must lie down some afternoons
and cry hard for whoever used

to make them happiest,
and wonder how their lives

have carried them
this far without ever once

explaining anything. I don't know
why I'm walking out here

with my coat darkening
and my boots sinking in, coming up

with a mild sucking sound
I like to hear. I don't care

where those girls are now.
Whatever they've made of it

they can have. Today I want
to resolve nothing.

I only want to walk
a little longer in the cold

blessing of the rain,
and lift my face to it.

Generations

Somewhere a shop of hanging meats,
shop of stink and blood, block and cleaver;

somewhere an immigrant, grandfather, stranger
with my last name. That man

untying his apron in 1910, scrubbing off
the pale fat, going home past brownstones

and churches, past vendors, streetcars, arias,
past the clatter of supper dishes, going home

to his new son, my father –
What is he to me, butcher with sausage fingers,

old Italian leaning over a child somewhere
in New York City, somewhere alive, what is he

that I go back to look for him, years after his death
and my father's death, knowing only

a name, a few scraps my father fed me?
My father who shortened that name, who hacked off

three lovely syllables, who raised American children.
What is the past to me

that I have to go back, pronouncing that word
in the silence of a cemetery, what is this stone

coming apart in my hands like bread, name
I eat and expel? Somewhere the smell of figs

and brine, strung garlic, rosemary and olives;
somewhere that place. Somewhere a boat

rocking, crossing over, entering the harbor. I wait
on the dock, one face in a crowd of faces.

Families disembark and stream toward the city,
and though I walk among them for hours,

hungry, haunting the streets,
I can't tell which of them is mine.

Somewhere a steak is wrapped in thick paper,
somewhere my grandmother is laid in the earth,

and my young father shines shoes on a corner,
turning his back to the Old World, forgetting.

I walk the night city, looking up at lit windows,
and there is no table set for me, nowhere

I can go to be filled. This is the city
of grandparents, immigrants, arrivals,

where I've come too late with my name,
an empty plate. This is the place.

Near Heron Lake

During the night, horses passed close
to our parked van. Inside I woke cold
under the sleeping bag, hearing their heavy sway,
the gravel harsh under their hooves as they moved off
down the bank to the river. You slept on,
though maybe in your dream you felt them enter
our life just long enough to cause that slight
stirring, a small spasm in your limbs and then
a sigh so quiet, so close to being nothing
but the next breath, I could believe you never guessed
how those huge animals broke out of the dark and came
toward us. Or how afraid I was before I understood
what they were – only horses, not anything
that would hurt us. The next morning
I watched you at the edge of the river
washing your face, your bare chest beaded with bright water,
and knew how much we needed this,
the day ahead with its calm lake
we would swim in, naked, able to touch again.
You were so beautiful. And I thought
the marriage might never end.

Collapsing Poem

The woman stands on the front steps, sobbing.
The man stays just inside the house,
leaning against the doorjamb. It's late, a wet
fog has left a sheer film over the windows
of cars along the street. The woman is drunk.
She begs the man, but he won't let her in.
Say it matters what happened between them;
say you can't judge whose fault this all is,
given the lack of context, given your own failures
with those you meant most to love.
Or maybe you don't care about them yet.
Maybe you need some way
to put yourself in this scene, some minor detail
that will make them seem so real you try to enter
this page to keep them from doing
to each other what you've done to someone,
somewhere: think about that for a minute,
while she keeps crying, and he speaks
in a voice so measured and calm he might be
talking to a child frightened by something
perfectly usual: darkness, thunder,
the coldness of the human heart.
But she's not listening, because now
she's hitting him, beating her fists against the chest
she laid her head on so many nights.
And by now, if you've been moved, it's because
you're thinking with regret of the person
this poem set out to remind you of,
and what you want more than anything is what
the man in the poem wants: for her to shut up.
And if you could only drive down that street
and emerge from the fog, maybe you
could get her to stop, but I can't do it.

All I can do is stand at that open door
making things worse. That's my talent,
that's why this poem won't get finished unless
you drag me from it, away from that man;
for Christ's sake, hurry, just pull up and keep
the motor running and take me wherever you're going.

The Divorcee and Gin

I love the frosted pints you come in,
and the tall bottles with their uniformed men;
the bars where you're poured chilled
into shallow glasses, the taste of drowned olives
and the scrawled benches where I see you
passed impatiently from one mouth
to another, the bag twisted tight around
your neck, the hand that holds you
shaking a little from its need
which is the true source of desire, God, I love
what you do to me at night when we're alone,
how you wait for me to take you into me
until I'm so confused with you I can't
stand up anymore. I know you want me
helpless, each cell whimpering, and I give
you that, letting you have me just the way
you like it. And when you're finished
you turn your face to the wall while I curl
around you again, and enter another morning
with aspirin and the useless ache
that comes from loving, too well,
those who, under the guise of pleasure,
destroy everything they touch.

Intimacy

The woman in the café making my cappuccino – dark eyes, dyed
      red hair,
sleeveless black turtleneck – used to be lovers with the man I'm
      seeing now.
She doesn't know me; we're strangers, but still I can't glance at her
casually, as I used to, before I knew. She stands at the machine,
      sinking the nozzle
into a froth of milk, staring at nothing – I don't know what she's
      thinking.
For all I know she might be remembering my lover, remembering
      whatever happened
between them – he's never told me, except to say that it wasn't
      important, and then
he changed the subject quickly, too quickly now that I think about it;
      might he,
after all, have been lying, didn't an expression of pain cross his face
      for just
an instant? I can't be sure. And really it was nothing, I tell myself;
there's no reason for me to feel awkward standing here, or
      complicitous,
as though there's something significant between us.
She could be thinking of anything; why, now, do I have the sudden
      suspicion
that she knows, that she feels me studying her, trying to imagine
      them together? –
her lipstick's dark red, darker than her hair – trying to see him
      kissing her, turning her over in bed
the way he likes to have me. I wonder if maybe
there were things about her he preferred, things he misses now that
      we're together;
sometimes, when he and I are making love, there are moments
I'm overwhelmed by sadness, and though I'm there with him I can't
      help thinking

of my ex-husband's hands, which I especially loved, and I want to
     go back
to that old intimacy, which often felt like the purest happiness
I'd ever known, or would. But all that's over; and besides, weren't
     there other lovers
who left no trace? When I see them now, I can barely remember
what they looked like undressed, or how it felt to have them
inside me. So what is it I feel as she pours the black espresso into
     the milk,
and pushes the cup toward me, and I give her the money,
and our eyes meet for just a second, and our fingers touch?

Last Call

It's the hour when everyone's drunk
and the bar turns marvelous, music
swirling over the red booths,
smoke rising from neglected cigarettes as in each glass
ice slides into other ice, dissolving;
it's when one stranger nudges another
and says, staring at the blurred rows of pour spouts,
I hear they banned dwarf tossing in France,
and the second man nods
and lays his head on the bar's slick surface,
not caring if he dies there, wanting, in fact, to die there
among the good friends he's just met, his cheek
in a wet pool of spilled beer.
It's when the woman in the corner gets up
and wobbles to the middle of the room,
leaving her blouse draped over a stool. Someone is buying
the house a final round, the cabs are being summoned,
and the gods that try to save us from ourselves
are taking us by the neck, gently,
and dropping us into the night; it's the hour
of the blind, and the dead, of lost loves
who come to claim you, finally, holding open
the swinging door, repeating over and over
a name that must be yours.

The Promise

When my daughter confessed she'd wanted to end her life at ten –
stepped out on the window ledge and stood there, at the edge

of a decision – we promised never to kill ourselves, never
to abandon each other. And I've never told her about the night

two years later when I came to a place in myself
where it seemed, for the first time, possible –

the way a door appears suddenly in a fairy tale, where the wall was
    solid.
I knew I could do it – I was drinking

and heartsick, I had enough pills.
I sat on my bed, arms around my knees,

and rocked the way I used to as a child.
Then, I'd believed in God; I would talk to Him

half the night sometimes, knowing
He was there, in heaven, just above the ceiling of my parents' room.

But now there was no one. Only
a couple of cats, locked together in some yard or alley, yowling

until someone raised a window, yelled and slammed it shut.
What a mess I was. How fiercely I loved her.

The Body in Extremis

First I think of it as a factory
where the foreman's passed out drunk
in his high room with the little window
while the radio slides into static
and down below no one gives a shit
about pride in labor considering what they're paid
so one by one they're taking off
their goggles and aprons and building a huge
bonfire in the center of the room and banging
the metal carts against one another while a few
holdouts stay grimly at their tasks
and try to ignore the din. But all that's
mechanical and wrong so I close my eyes
to try again: your body is a vase of flowers,
their brown stalks slick in the fetid water,
the shrunken tissue of the petals falling
on a scarred table beside an old couch –
stained, burn-holed – a sunken shape in a darkened
living room. Outside is the worst
section of the city, figures hurrying into doorways,
up to no good, random gunshots and exploding glass,
alarms, alarms – amazing what the mind can do
and still fail to absorb the plain fact
of you, railed-in and dying.
In this nearly sterile room
there are no more ways to imagine
your thin form beneath the covers, your face
I now bend close to kiss,
and whatever I make of the grief
that's coming, it won't change this, *this*.

Rain

is what I can't bear going on & not
easing all day hitting the windows like someone
throwing shovelfuls of dirt onto a
coffin keeping me in bed sick but not physically only
reading a poet's lines about Vietnam thinking of
Harry & Danny & Ron how long ago it was now
I don't know them or only my body remembers
lying beneath Harry on the hard
ground of the field frozen with little stars
of frost his hands holding an M16 or a woman
with black hair or my shoulders as he
came inside me crying & Danny strapping on
his wooden leg to teach me karate saying *Don't*
be afraid to maim his naked thigh scarred
& oddly beautiful & his one foot the divot of flesh gouged
out or Ron talking bitterly about America & the night
I pushed his wheelchair too fast ran it
off the sidewalk into a tree & we laughed &
how I'd grow so tired of listening to him & never
knowing if he cared what I thought all of it
gone into my history of loss a litany I need
to sing I don't know why today it's just the rain
keeps up & I feel so cold inside I can't get out
of bed or understand why these ghosts
of men come back to press me down I couldn't
help them or I did maybe a little tenderness a
breast or kiss what I could offer not knowing I was
so young believing I could heal them the rain
relentless against the windows when will it stop oh when

Tell Me

I am going to stop thinking about my losses now
and listen to yours. I'm so sick of dragging them

with me wherever I go, like children up too late
who should be curled in their own beds

under the only blanket that warms them.
I am going to send them home while I stay

at this party all night with the loud music pumping
and the dancers moving gracelessly under the lights

and the drinkers spilling their scotches on their sleeves.
I am going to join them. I'm going to drink until

I'm so wasted I forget I have children, I'll dance
until I ache, until I make a spectacle of myself.

So tell me. Tell me how you hurt
even though I can't help you. Tell me

their ages, how they keep you up nights,
how sometimes you wish they were dead

but keep finding yourself gazing at them
tenderly while they sleep. Then, please, dance with me,

hold me while we fool ourselves
they aren't out there, pressing their damp

hollow faces to the windows. Tell me
that if we kiss a new one won't start to slip

from each of us, tell me you can't already feel
the little hole burning in your side

or to hear the others moving over to make room,
shrieking and clapping with joy.

Mermaid Song

(for Aya at fifteen)

Damp-haired from the bath, you drape yourself
upside down across the sofa, reading,
one hand idly sunk into a bowl
of crackers, goldfish with smiles stamped on.
I think they are growing gills, swimming
up the sweet air to reach you. Small girl,
my slim miracle, they multiply.
In the black hours when I lie sleepless,
near drowning, dread-heavy, your face
is the bright lure I look for, love's hook
piercing me, hauling me cleanly up.

Onset

Watching that frenzy of insects above the bush of white flowers,
bush I see everywhere on hill after hill, all I can think of
is how terrifying spring is, in its tireless, mindless replications.
Everywhere emergence: seed case, chrysalis, uterus, endless
      manufacturing.
And the wrapped stacks of Styrofoam cups in the grocery, lately
I can't stand them, the shelves of canned beans and soups, freezers
of identical dinners; then the snowflake-diamond-snowflake of the rug
beneath my chair, rows of books turning their backs,
even my two feet, how they mirror each other oppresses me,
the way they fit so perfectly together, how I can nestle one big toe
      into the other
like little continents that have drifted; my God the unity of everything,
my hands and eyes, yours; doesn't that frighten you sometimes,
      remembering
the pleasure of nakedness in fresh sheets, all the lovers there before you,
beside you, crowding you out? And the scouring griefs,
don't look at them all or they'll kill you, you can barely encompass
      your own;
I'm saying I know all about you, whoever you are, it's spring
and it's starting again, the longing that begins, and begins, and begins.

'What Do Women Want?'

I want a red dress.
I want it flimsy and cheap,
I want it too tight, I want to wear it
until someone tears it off me.
I want it sleeveless and backless,
this dress, so no one has to guess
what's underneath. I want to walk down
the street past Thrifty's and the hardware store
with all those keys glittering in the window,
past Mr and Mrs Wong selling day-old
donuts in their café, past the Guerra brothers
slinging pigs from the truck and onto the dolly,
hoisting the slick snouts over their shoulders.
I want to walk like I'm the only
woman on earth and I can have my pick.
I want that red dress bad.
I want it to confirm
your worst fears about me,
to show you how little I care about you
or anything except what
I want. When I find it, I'll pull that garment
from its hanger like I'm choosing a body
to carry me into this world, through
the birth-cries and the love-cries too,
and I'll wear it like bones, like skin,
it'll be the goddamned
dress they bury me in.

Good Girl

Look at you, sitting there being good.
After two years you're still dying for a cigarette.
And not drinking on weekdays, who thought that one up?
Don't you want to run to the corner right now
for a fifth of vodka and have it with cranberry juice
and a nice lemon slice, wouldn't the backyard
that you're so sick of staring out into
look better then, the tidy yard your landlord tends
day and night – the fence with its fresh coat of paint,
the ash-free barbecue, the patio swept clean of small twigs-
don't you want to mess it all up, to roll around
like a dog in his flower beds? Aren't you a dog anyway,
always groveling for love and begging to be petted?
You ought to get into the garbage and lick the insides
of the can, the greasy wrappers, the picked-over bones;
you ought to drive your snout into the coffee grounds.
Ah, coffee! Why not gulp some down with four cigarettes
and then blast naked into the streets, and leap on the first
beautiful man you find? The words *Ruin me*, haven't they
been jailed in your throat for forty years, isn't it time
you set them loose in slutty dresses and torn fishnets
to totter around in five-inch heels and smeared mascara?
Sure it's time. You've rolled over long enough.
Forty, forty-one. At the end of all this
there's one lousy biscuit, and it tastes like dirt.
So get going. Listen, they're howling for you now:
up and down the block your neighbors' dogs
burst into frenzied barking and won't shut up.

Physics

In the darkness of the booth, you have to find
the slot blindly and fumble the quarter in. The black
shade goes up. Now there's a naked woman

dancing before you and you're looking
at her knees, then raising your eyes
to the patch of wiry hair which she obligingly parts

with two fingers while her other hand
palms her body from breast to hip
and it's you doing it, for a second

you're touching her like that and when
you lift your face to hers she's not
gazing into space as you expected but

looking back, right at you, with an expression
that says *I love you, I belong to you compl—*
but then the barrier descends. You shove

another quarter in, but the thing has to close down
before slowly opening again like a pupil adjusting
to the absence of light and by the time it does

you've lost her. She's moved on to the next
low window holding someone's blurred face,
and another woman is coming nearer

under the stage lights and in the mirrors,
looking so happy to see you trapped there
like some poor fish in a plastic baggie

that will finally be released into a small bowl
with a ceramic castle and a few colored rocks,
and you open your mouth just like a fish waiting

for the flakes of food, understanding nothing
of what causes them to rain down
upon you. You can feel your hunger sharpening

as she thrusts herself over and over into
the air between you. And now, unbelievably,
there comes into your mind

not the image of fucking her
but an explanation you heard once
of what vast distances exist

between any two electrons. Suppose,
the scientist said, the atom were the size
of an orange; then imagine that orange as big

as the earth. The electrons inside it
would be only the size of cherries. *Cherries,*
you think, and inserting your quarter you see one

sitting on an ice floe in the Antarctic, a pinprick
of blood, and another in a village in Northern Africa
being rolled on the tongue of a dusty child

while the dancer shakes her breasts at you,
displaying nipples you know you'll never
bite into in this lifetime; all you can do

is hold tight to the last useless coins
and repeat to yourself that they're solid,
they're definitely solid, you can definitely feel them.

Aliens

Now that you're finally happy
you notice how sad your friends are.
One calls you from a pay phone, crying.
Her husband has cancer; only a few months,
maybe less, before his body gives in.
She's tired all the time, can barely eat.
What can you say that will help her?
You yourself are ravenous.
You come so intensely with your new lover
you wonder if you've turned
into someone else. Maybe an alien
has taken over your body
in order to experience the good life
here on earth: dark rum and grapefruit juice,
fucking on the kitchen floor,
then showering together and going out
to eat and eat. When your friends call –
the woman drinking too much, the one who lost
her brother, the ex-lover whose right ear
went dead and then began buzzing –
the alien doesn't want to listen.
More food, it whines. *Fuck me again,*
it whispers, *and afterward we'll go to the circus.*
The phone rings. *Don't answer it.*
You reach for a fat eclair,
bite into it while the room fills
with aliens – wandering, star-riddled creatures
who vibrate in the rapturous air,
longing to come down and join you,
looking for a place they can rest.

Like That

Love me like a wrong turn on a bad road late at night, with no moon
    and no town anywhere
and a large hungry animal moving heavily through the brush in the
    ditch.
Love me with a blindfold over your eyes and the sound of rusty water
blurting from the faucet in the kitchen, leaking down through
the floorboards to hot cement. Do it without asking,
without wondering or thinking anything, while the machinery's
shut down and the watchman's slumped asleep before his small TV
showing the empty garage, the deserted hallways, while the thieves
    slice through
the fence with steel clippers. Love me when you can't find
a decent restaurant open anywhere, when you're alone in a glaring
    diner
with two nuns arguing in the back booth, when your eggs are greasy
and your hash browns underdone. Snick the buttons off the front of
    my dress
and toss them one by one into the pond where carp lurk just beneath
    the surface,
their cold fins waving. Love me on the hood of a truck no one's
    driven
in years, sunk to its fenders in weeds and dead sunflowers;
and in the lilies, your mouth on my white throat, while turtles drag
their bellies through slick mud, through the footprints of coots and
    ducks.
Do it when no one's looking, when the riots begin and the planes
    open up,
when the bus leaps the curb and the driver hits the brakes and the
    pedal sinks to the floor,
while someone hurls a plate against the wall and picks up another,
love me like a freezing shot of vodka, like pure agave, love me
when you're lonely, when we're both too tired to speak, when you
    don't believe

in anything, listen, there isn't anything, it doesn't matter; lie down
with me and close your eyes, the road curves here, I'm cranking up
    the radio
and we're going, we won't turn back as long as you love me,
as long as you keep on doing it exactly like that.

Prayer

Sometimes, when we're lying after love,
I look at you and see your body's future
of lying beneath the earth; putting the heel
of my hand against your rib I feel how faint
and far away the heartbeat is. I rest
my cheek against your left nipple and listen
to the surge of blood, seeing your life splashed out,
filmy water hurled from a pot
onto dry grass. And I want to be pressed
deep into the bed and covered over,
the way a seed is pressed into a hole,
the dirt tamped down with a trowel.
I want to be a failed seed, the kind
that doesn't grow, that doesn't know it's meant to.
I want to lie here without moving, lifeless
as an animal that's slaughtered, its blood smeared
on a doorpost, I want death to take me if it
has to, to spare you, I want it to pass over.

One-Night Stands

Those men I fucked when I was drunk,
I can't even see their faces anymore.
Or the shape of their hands, hard
bones of their hips knocking against me,
curve of an ass or shoulder. Whatever
I tasted as they slid over me, nameless,
whatever words they tongued into me,
I don't have them. What I have
are the bars I met them in, the sweat
on a glass of beer, the dense granules of red
or blue light sifting toward me, sharp swell
of music and a voice saying *Let's get out
of here.* We always went to a place
I'd never be able to find again
if I ever bothered to look.
There are people we're meant
to lose, moments that rinse off.
And there are still nights I lie awake
with the pulse, the throb,
that says *Let's go
somewhere and watch the moon rise
over three rows of bottles and a cash register.
Let someone else pay. Ask for a cigarette
and the fire to light it, burn a few hours,
show me you love me that much.*

For Desire

Give me the strongest cheese, the one that stinks best;
and I want the good wine, the swirl in crystal
surrendering the bruised scent of blackberries,
or cherries, the rich spurt in the back
of the throat, the holding it there before swallowing.
Give me the lover who yanks open the door
of his house and presses me to the wall
in the dim hallway, and keeps me there until I'm drenched
and shaking, whose kisses arrive by the boatload
and begin their delicious diaspora
through the cities and small towns of my body.
To hell with the saints, with the martyrs
of my childhood meant to instruct me
in the power of endurance and faith,
to hell with the next world and its pallid angels
swooning and sighing like Victorian girls.
I want this world. I want to walk into
the ocean and feel it trying to drag me along
like I'm nothing but a broken bit of scratched glass,
and I want to resist it. I want to go
staggering and flailing my way
through the bars and back rooms,
through the gleaming hotels and the weedy
lots of abandoned sunflowers and the parks
where dogs are let off their leashes
in spite of the signs, where they sniff each
other and roll together in the grass, I want to
lie down somewhere and suffer for love until
it nearly kills me, and then I want to get up again
and put on that little black dress and wait
for you, yes you, to come over here
and get down on your knees and tell me
just how fucking good I look.

Flood

How images enter you, the shutter of the body
clicking when you're not even looking:
smooth chill of satin sheets, piano keys, a pastry's glazy crust
floating up, suddenly, so the hairs along your arm
lift in that current of memory, and your tongue tastes
the sweet salt of a lover as he surges
against you, plunges toward the place you can't
dive into but which is deepening each moment
you are alive, the black pupil widening,
the man going down and in, the food and
champagne and music and light, there is no bottom to this,
silt and murk of losses that won't ever settle,
and the huge unsleeping fish, voracious for pleasure,
and the soundless fathoms where nothing
yet exists, this minute, the next, the last
breath let out and not returning, oh hold
on to me as the waters rise, don't be afraid,
we are going to join the others, we are going
to remember and tell them everything.

What Is This Thing Called Love

(2004)

First Kiss

Afterwards you had that drunk, drugged look
my daughter used to get, when she had let go
of my nipple, her mouth gone slack and her eyes
turned vague and filmy, as though behind them
the milk was rising up to fill her
whole head, that would loll on the small
white stalk of her neck so I would have to hold her
closer, amazed at the sheer power
of satiety, which was nothing like the needing
to be fed, the wild flailing and crying until she fastened
herself to me and made the seal tight
between us, and sucked, drawing the liquid down and
out of my body; no, *this* was the crowning
moment, this giving of herself, knowing
she could show me how helpless
she was – that's what I saw, that night when you
pulled your mouth from mine and
leaned back against a chain link fence,
in front of a burned-out church: a man
who was going to be that vulnerable,
that easy and impossible to hurt.

Stolen Moments

What happened, happened once. So now it's best
in memory – an orange he sliced: the skin
unbroken, then the knife, the chilled wedge
lifted to my mouth, his mouth, the thin
membrane between us, the exquisite orange,
tongue, orange, my nakedness and his,
the way he pushed me up against the fridge –
Now I get to feel his hands again, the kiss
that didn't last, but sent some neural twin
flashing wildly through the cortex. Love's
merciless, the way it travels in
and keeps emitting light. Beside the stove
we ate an orange. And there were purple flowers
on the table. And we still had hours.

Blues for Dante Alighieri

...without hope we live on in desire...
INFERNO, IV

Our room was too small, the sheets scratchy and hot –
Our room was a kind of hell, we thought,
and killed a half-liter of Drambuie we'd bought.

We walked over the Arno and back across.
We walked all day, and in the evening, lost,
argued and wandered in circles. At last

we found our hotel. The next day we left for Rome.
We found the Intercontinental, and a church full of bones,
and ate takeout Chinese in our suite, alone.

It wasn't a great journey, only a side trip.
It wasn't love for eternity, or any such crap;
it was just something that happened...

We packed suitcases, returned the rental car.
We packed souvenirs, repaired to the airport bar
and talked about pornography, and movie stars.

So What

Guess what. If love is only chemistry—
phenylethylamine, that molecule
that dizzies up the brain's back room, smoky
with hot bebop, it won't be long until
a single worker's mopping up the scuffed
and littered floor, whistling tunelessly,
each endorphin cooling like a snuffed
glass candle, the air stale with memory.
So what, you say; outside, a shadow lifts
a trumpet from its case, lifts it like an ingot
and scatters a few virtuosic riffs
toward the locked-down stores. You've quit
believing that there's more, but you're still stirred
enough to stop, and wait, listening hard.

Muse

When I walk in,
men buy me drinks before I even reach the bar.

They fall in love with me after one night,
even if we never touch.

I tell you I've got this shit down to a science.

They sweat with my memory,
alone in cheap rooms they listen

to moans through the wall
and wonder if that's me,

letting out a scream as the train whines by.

But I'm already two states away, lying with a boy
I let drink rain from the pulse at my throat.

No one leaves me, I'm the one that chooses.
I show up like money on the sidewalk.

Listen, baby. Those are my high heels dangling from the phone wire.

I'm the crow flapping down,
that's my black slip

you catch sight of when the pain
twists into you so deep

you have to close your eyes and weep like a goddamned woman.

You Don't Know What Love Is

but you know how to raise it in me
like a dead girl winched up from a river. How to
wash off the sludge, the stench of our past.
How to start clean. This love even sits up
and blinks; amazed, she takes a few shaky steps.
Any day now she'll try to eat solid food. She'll want
to get into a fast car, one low to the ground, and drive
to some cinderblock shithole in the desert
where she can drink and get sick and then
dance in nothing but her underwear. You know
where she's headed, you know she'll wake up
with an ache she can't locate and no money
and a terrible thirst. So to hell
with your warm hands sliding inside my shirt
and your tongue down my throat
like an oxygen tube. Cover me
in black plastic. Let the mourners through.

Ex-Boyfriends

They hang around, hitting on your friends
or else you never hear from them again.
They call when they're drunk, or finally get sober,

they're passing through town and want dinner,
they take your hand across the table, kiss you
when you come back from the bathroom.

They were your loves, your victims,
your good dogs or bad boys, and they're over
you now. One writes a book in which a woman

who sounds suspiciously like you
is the first to be sadistically dismembered
by a serial killer. They're getting married

and want you to be the first to know,
or they've been fired and need a loan,
their new girlfriend hates you,

they say they don't miss you but show up
in your dreams, calling to you from the shoeboxes
where they're buried in rows in your basement.

Some nights you find one floating into bed with you,
propped on an elbow, giving you a look
of fascination, a look that says *I can't believe*

I've found you. It's the same way
your current boyfriend gazed at you last night,
before he pulled the plug on the tiny white lights

above the bed, and moved against you in the dark
broken occasionally by the faint restless arcs
of headlights from the freeway's passing trucks,

the big rigs that travel and travel,
hauling their loads between cities, warehouses,
following the familiar routes of their loneliness.

Death Poem

Do I have to bring it up again, isn't there another subject?
Can I forget about the scrap of flattened squirrel fur
fluttering on the road, can I forget the road
and how I can't stop driving no matter what,
not even for gas, or love, can I please not think
about my father left in some town behind me,
in his blue suit, with his folded hands,
and my grandmother moaning about her bladder
and swallowing all the pills, and the towns I'm passing now
can I try not to see them, the children squatting
by the ditches, the holes in their chests and foreheads,
the woman cradling her tumor, the dog dragging its crippled hips?
I can close my eyes and sit back if I want to,
I can lean against my friends' shoulders
and eat as they're eating, and drink from the bottle
being passed back and forth; I can lighten up, can't I,
Christ, can't I? There is another subject, in a minute
I'll think of it. I will. And if you know it, help me.
Help me. Remind me why I'm here.

Scary Movies

Today the cloud shapes are terrifying,
and I keep expecting some enormous
black-and-white B-movie Cyclops
to appear at the edge of the horizon,

to come striding over the ocean
and drag me from my kitchen
to the deep cave that flickered
into my young brain one Saturday

at the Baronet Theater where I sat helpless
between my older brothers, pumped up
on candy and horror – that cave,
the litter of human bones

gnawed on and flung toward the entrance,
I can smell their stench as clearly
as the bacon fat from breakfast.
This is how it feels to lose it –

not sanity, I mean, but whatever it is
that helps you get up in the morning
and actually leave the house
on those days when it seems like death

in his brown uniform
is cruising his panel truck
of packages through your neighborhood.
I think of a friend's voice

on her answering machine –
Hi, I'm not here –
the morning of her funeral,
the calls filling up the tape

and the mail still arriving,
and I feel as afraid as I was
after all those vampire movies
when I'd come home and lie awake

all night, rigid in my bed,
unable to get up
even to pee because the undead
were waiting underneath it;

if I so much as stuck a bare
foot out there in the unprotected air
they'd grab me by the ankle and pull me
under. And my parents said there was

nothing there, when I was older
I would know better, and now
they're dead, and I'm older,
and I know better.

Dead Girls

show up often in the movies, facedown
in the weeds beside the highway.
Kids find them by the river, or in the woods,

under leaves, one pink-nailed hand thrust up.
Detectives stand over them in studio apartments
or lift their photos off pianos

in the houses they almost grew up in.
A dead girl can kick a movie into gear
better than a saloon brawl, better

than a factory explosion, just
by lying there. Anyone can play her,
any child off the street

can be hog-tied and dumped from a van
or strangled blue in a kitchen, a bathroom,
an alley, a school. That's the beauty

of a dead girl. Even a plain one
who feels worthless
as a clod of dirt, broken

by the sorrow of gazing all day
at a fashion magazine,
can be made whole, redeemed

by what she finally can't help being,
the center of attention, the special,
desirable, dead, dead girl.

Eating Together

I know my friend is going,
though she still sits there
across from me in the restaurant,
and leans over the table to dip
her bread in the oil on my plate; I know
how thick her hair used to be,
and what it takes for her to discard
her man's cap partway through our meal,
to look straight at the young waiter
and smile when he asks
how we are liking it. She eats
as though starving – chicken, dolmata,
the buttery flakes of filo –
and what's killing her
eats, too. I watch her lift
a glistening black olive and peel
the meat from the pit, watch
her fine long fingers, and her face,
puffy from medication. She lowers
her eyes to the food, pretending
not to know what I know. She's going.
And we go on eating.

Cat Poem

The cat's hardly moving; she's stopped eating, stopped shitting,
    she puts her face to a bowl of water
but doesn't drink. My friend says not to write about her, he says
    no one wants to read about my pet
so let's say it's your cat, not mine, or maybe you have a dog; even I,
    a cat owner, think that dogs
are superior, they have such compassionate eyes. Once, an actor –
    not just any actor, but Al Pacino –
did an entire stage performance keeping in mind the liquid brown
    eyes of someone
in the audience, playing to those eyes, and when the house lights
    went up he realised
it was a guide dog, a German Shepherd, so maybe if you imagine
    your dog or even better
Al Pacino's dog, hardly moving, its ribs heaving, that would be
    preferable, but if you don't
like dogs maybe a bird will do, or whales, people seem to care
    about the whales, lying on their great sides
on the beach, or the seals with their skulls crushed by clubs –
    think of them, their orphaned pups –
or just forget about the animals entirely; forget the beagles smoking
    while they run on treadmills
and those rabbits the cosmetic companies seem to favor, though
    it's harder to discount
the chimpanzees injected with simian AIDS, unless maybe the
    retrovirus inhabiting your friend
has just become immune to the protease inhibitors, so forget the
    chimpanzees, too,
remember my cat? She's lying on the bathroom rug, her organs
    shutting down – imagine I wept
all day for her – Vanilla is her name, my daughter named her at
    five, now my daughter's grown,

now the cat's old, I've put her on the bed and I'm talking to her,
    saying It's all right,
go if you need to, and I'm watching death – he's stroking her fur,
    making his rounds,
he's talking to her softly, telling her to stop, ignoring me for now,
    ignoring you.

February 14

This is a valentine for the surgeons
ligating the portal veins and hepatic artery,
placing vascular clamps on the vena cava
as my brother receives a new liver.

And a valentine for each nurse;
though I don't know how many there are
leaning over him in their gauze masks,
I'm sure I have enough – as many hearts

as it takes, as much embarrassing sentiment
as anyone needs. One heart
for the sutures, one for the instruments
I don't know the names of,

and the monitors and lights,
and the gloves slippery with his blood
as the long hours pass,
as a T-tube is placed to drain the bile.

And one heart for the donor,
who never met my brother
but who understood the body as gift
and did not want to bury or burn that gift.

For that man, I can't imagine how
one heart could suffice. But I offer it.
While my brother lies sedated,
opened from sternum to groin,

I think of a dead man, being remembered
by others in their sorrow, and I offer him
these words of praise and gratitude,
oh beloved whom we did not know.

It

I can still remember that sensation of being shaken
by something that gripped me and wouldn't let go
until my daughter was born, sliding toward the blanket
spread on the floor where I squatted,
the doctor squatting, too, waiting to catch her,
until she was completely outside of me
and the creature – thing – that had held me helpless
simply dropped me and turned away,
as though I were no longer interesting to it,
or tasted bad, as though suddenly remembering
urgent business elsewhere. And I felt I was again
the agent of my life; it was mine, and the new life
laid on my stomach after I'd staggered to the bed
was mine, too, I would have to learn
what she needed and how not to harm her.
But how could I protect her
from whatever had mastered me so completely,
opening my body ruthlessly to bring her down
into this world, how could I keep her
from that thing if it wanted to unmake her?
That morning of her birth I felt it close to me,
forcing out the sweat and screams, and I knew
it would have killed me if it had to, for her sake,
for those few hours it loved her
like a mother, as it had once loved me in order to get me out.

The Way of the World

We know the ugly hate the beautiful,
and the bitter losers are all seething
over bad coffee, washed in the sleazy fluorescence
of fast-food restaurants. We know

the wheelchairs hate the shoes,
and the medicines envy the vitamins,
which is why sometimes a whole bottle
of sleeping pills will gather like a wave

and rush down someone's throat to drown
in the sour ocean of the stomach.
And let's not even mention the poor,
since hardly anyone does.

It's the way of the world –
the sorrowful versus the happy,
and the stupid against everyone,
especially themselves. So don't pretend

you're glad when your old friends
get lucky in work, or love,
while you're still drifting through life
like a lobster in a restaurant tank. Go on,

admit it: you'd claw them to death
if you could. But you're helpless,
knocking futiley against clear glass you can't
break through. They're opening champagne,

oblivious of you, just as you don't notice
how many backs you've scrambled over
to get this far, your black eyes glittering,
your slow limbs grimly and steadily working.

Chicken

Why did she cross the road?
She should have stayed in her little cage,
shat upon by her sisters above her,
shitting on her sisters below her.

God knows how she got out.
God sees everything. God has his eye
on the chicken, making her break
like the convict headed for the river,

sloshing his way through the water
to throw off the dogs, raising
his arms to starlight to praise
whatever isn't locked in a cell.

He'll make it to a farmhouse
where kind people will feed him.
They'll bring green beans and bread,
home-brewed hops. They'll bring

the chicken the farmer found
by the side of the road, dazed
from being clipped by a pickup,
whose delicate brain stem

he snapped with a twist,
whose asshole his wife stuffed
with rosemary and a lemon wedge.
Everything has its fate,

but only God knows what that is.
The spirit of the chicken will enter the convict.
Sometimes, in his boxy apartment,
listening to his neighbors above him,

annoying his neighbors below him,
he'll feel a terrible hunger
and an overwhelming urge
to jab his head at the television over and over.

Lush Life

In this bottle a searing headache,
in that one a car angling off the road
to meet a tree in your neighbor's yard,

in the next one a man who removes
your clothes while you spin
down into the whirlpool of the bed's black sheets.

At the bottom of another: locked metal box
you can't pry open, though you can hear
someone in there, muttering and crying

and saying how sorry she is.
And don't forget the worm of shame
that uncurls in your throat sometimes,

and the bathrooms where you crouched
shaking before a toilet, your hair limp,
the sour evening rising up inside you.

So what are you doing, sitting there
holding a half-full highball glass,
listening to the jazz of ice, the slow blues

of a just-lit cigarette? Some low voice
is crooning your name, and in the double
being poured behind the bar

the tenor sax is starting its solo, taking you
out over the changes, sounding
just like love, just like it won't ever stop.

Bad Girl

She's the one sleeping all day, in a room
at the back of your brain. She wakes up
at the sound of a cork twisted free
of a bottle, a stabbed olive

plopped into gin. She's prettier than you
and right now you bore the shit out of her,
sitting there sipping when she wants
to stand on the rim of the glass, naked,

dive straight to the bottom and lie there
looking up, amazed at how the world
wavers and then comes clear. You're not
going to let her. You've locked her in

with her perfume and cheap novels,
her deep need for trouble. She's the one
calling to you through the keyhole,
then sneaking away to squirm out

a window and tear her silk dress.
You can't guess where she's going,
or who you'll wake up with
when you finally wake up,

your head throbbing like a heart.
She's the one you're scared of,
the one who dares you to go ahead
and completely disappear. It's not

you the boys are noticing, not you
turning toward them and throwing off light.
You're crouched in a corner, coming undone.
She's in love with you now. She's the one.

Blues for Robert Johnson

Give me a pint of whiskey with a broken seal
Give me one more hour with a broken feel
I can't sleep again and a black dog's on my trail

You're singing hell hound, crossroad, love in vain
You're singing, and the black sky is playing rain
You're stomping your feet, shaking the windowpane

I put my palm to the glass to get the cold
I drink the memories that scald
Drink to the loves that failed and failed

Look down into the river, I can see you there
Looking down into the blue light of a woman's hair
Saying to her *Baby, dark gon' catch me here*

You're buried in Mississippi under a stone
You're buried and still singing under the ground
And the blues fell mama's child, tore me all upside down

Fuck

There are people who will tell you
that using the word *fuck* in a poem
indicates a serious lapse
of taste, or imagination,

or both. It's vulgar,
indecorous, an obscenity
that crashes down like an anvil
falling through a skylight

to land on a restaurant table,
on the white linen, the cut-glass vase of lilacs.
But if you were sitting
over coffee when the metal

hit your saucer like a missile,
wouldn't that be the first thing
you'd say? Wouldn't you leap back
shouting, or at least thinking it,

over and over, bell-note riotously clanging
in the church of your brain
while the solicitous waiter
led you away, wouldn't you prop

your shaking elbows on the bar
and order your first drink in months,
telling yourself you were lucky
to be alive? And if you wouldn't

say anything but *Mercy* or *Oh my*
or *Land sakes*, well then
I don't want to know you anyway
and I don't give a fuck what you think

131

of my poem. The world is divided
into those whose opinions matter
and those who will never have
a clue, and if you knew

which one you were I could talk
to you, and tell you that sometimes
there's only one word that means
what you need it to mean, the way

there's only one person
when you first fall in love,
or one infant's cry that calls forth
the burning milk, one name

that you pray to when prayer
is what's left to you. I'm saying
in the beginning was the word
and it was good, it meant one human

entering another and it's still
what I love, the word made
flesh. *Fuck me*, I say to the one
whose lovely body I want close,

and as we fuck I know it's holy,
a psalm, a hymn, a hammer
ringing down on an anvil,
forging a whole new world.

Augury

That girl in the stilettos and tight dress
    is my girl, parading back and forth
        before my closet

in the precarious shoes she bought for the prom.
    She thinks she has to practice being sexy. She can't
        imagine the future

I can see so clearly: over the calm sea
    of the mirror, a thousand warriors set out,
        ready to kill

or die for the sake of her beauty.
    I can see how the tiny sails will disappear
        into the distance,

looking like they're going under, swallowed
    by some jealous god or other. She stares intently
        at the mirror

but still she can't see the ships foundering,
    the hearts being dashed on the rocks. Now
        she smoothes glittery

shadow over her eyelids, dark lipstick
    on her mouth. When she blows a kiss
        a wind drags

the waves up to a great height, before
    they topple over and crush any man
        who's still alive.

Kisses

All the kisses I've ever been given, today I feel them on my mouth.
And my knees feel them, the reckless ones placed there
through the holes in my jeans while I sat on a car hood
or a broken sofa in somebody's basement, stoned, the way I was
in those days, still amazed that boys and even men would want to
lower their beautiful heads like horses drinking from a river and taste me.
The back of my neck feels them, my hair swept aside to expose the nape,
and my breasts tingle the way they did when my milk came in after the
      birth,
when I was swollen, and sleepless, and my daughter fed and fed until I
      pried
her from me and laid her in her crib. Even the chaste kisses that brushed
my cheeks, the fatherly ones on my forehead, I feel them rising up from
      underneath
the skin of the past, a delicate, roseate rash; and the ravishing ones, God,
I think of them and the filaments in my brain start buzzing crazily and
      flare out.
Every kiss is here somewhere, all over me like a fine, shiny grit, like I'm
      a pale
fish that's been dipped in a thick swirl of raw egg and dragged through
      flour,
slid down into a deep skillet, into burning. Today I know I've lost no one.
My loves are here: wrists, eyelids, damp toes, all scars, and my mouth
pouring praises, still asking, saying *kiss me*; when I'm dead kiss this poem,
it needs you to know it goes on, give it your lovely mouth, your living
      tongue.

Lucifer at the Starlite

(2009)

November 11

(2004)

O everyone's dead and the rain today is marvelous!
I drive to the gym, the streets are slick,
everyone's using their wipers, people are walking
with their shoulders hunched, wearing hoods
or holding up umbrellas, of course, of course,
it's all to be expected – fantastic!
My mother's friend Annie, her funeral's today!
The writer Iris Chang, she just shot herself!
And Arafat, he's dead, too! The doctors refuse
to say what killed him, his wife is fighting
with the Palestinians over his millions, the parking lot
of the gym is filled with muddy puddles!
I run 4.3 mph on the treadmill, and they're dead
in Baghdad and Fallujah, Mosul and Samarra and Latifiya –
Nadia and Surayah, Nahla and Hoda and Noor,
their husbands and cousins and brothers –
dead in their own neighborhoods! Imagine!
Marine Staff Sgt David G. Ries, 29, Clark, WA: killed!
Army Spc Quoc Binh Tran, 26, Mission Viejo, CA: killed,
Army Spc Bryan L. Freeman, 31, Lumberton, NJ – same deal!
Marine Lance Cpl Jeffrey Larn, 22, NY, you guessed it!
O I could go on and on, for as long as I live!
In Africa, too, they've been starved and macheted!
The morning paper said the Serbs apologised
for Srebrenica, 7,800 Muslims murdered in 1995,
I know it's old news, but hey, they're still dead!
I almost forgot my neighbor's niece, 16 and puking
in Kaiser Emergency, the cause a big mystery
until the autopsy – toxic shock syndrome,
of all things – I thought that was history, too,
but I guess girls are still dying; who knew! I run
for two miles, my knees hurt, and my shins,

I step off and stretch for a bit, I go back outside
into the rain, it feels chilly and good, it goes on
all day, unending and glorious, falling and filling
the roof gutters, flooding the low-lying roads.

For You

For you I undress down to the sheaths of my nerves.
I remove my jewelry and set it on the nightstand,
I unhook my ribs, spread my lungs flat on a chair.
I dissolve like a remedy in water, in wine.
I spill without staining, and leave without stirring the air.
I do it for love. For love, I disappear.

Lucifer at the Starlite

(after George Meredith)

Here's my bright idea for life on earth:
better management. The CEO
has lost touch with the details. I'm worth
as much, but I care; I come down here, I show
my face, I'm a real regular. A toast:
To our boys and girls in the war, grinding
through sand, to everybody here, our host
who's mostly mist, like methane rising
from retreating ice shelves. Put me in command.
For every town, we'll have a marching band.
For each thoroughbred, a comfortable stable;
for each worker, a place beneath the table.
For every forward step a stumbling.
A shadow over every starlit thing.

Storm Catechism

The gods are rinsing their just-boiled pasta
in a colander, which is why
it is humid and fitfully raining
down here in the steel sink of mortal life.
Sometimes you can smell the truffle oil
and hear the ambrosia being knocked back,
sometimes you catch a drift
of laughter in that thunder crack: Zeus
knocking over his glass, spilling lightning
into a tree. The tree shears away from itself
and falls on a car, killing a high school girl.
Or maybe it just crashes down
on a few trash cans, and the next day
gets cut up and hauled away by the city.
Either way, hilarity. The gods are infinitely perfect
as is their divine mac and cheese.
Where does macaroni come from? Where does matter?
Why does the cat act autistic when you call her,
then bat around a moth for an hour, watching intently
as it drags its wings over the area rug?
The gods were here first, and they're bigger.
They always were, and always will be
living it up in their father's mansion.
You only crawled from the drain
a few millennia ago,
after inventing legs for yourself
so you could stand, inventing fists
in order to raise them and curse the heavens.
Do the gods see us?
Will the waters be rising soon?
The waters will be rising soon.
Find someone or something to cling to.

Verities

Into every life a little ax must fall.
Every dog has its choke chain.
Every cloud has a shadow.
Better dead than fed.
He who laughs, will not last.
Sticks and stones will break you,
and then the names of things will be changed.
A stitch in time saves no one.
The darkest hour comes.

Long-Distance

Your wooden leg stood beside the bed
in its tennis shoe & sock, trailing its fasteners,

its amputated man leaning invisibly against the wall.
You pulled back the sheet so I could touch

your stump, the small hole in your left foot.
I touched everything. I was curious. I was eighteen

& ignorant. You told me the little
you thought I could handle.

Thirty years gone since then
to wives, meth, government checks…

Last year they took a kidney
& a few inches more of your right thigh.

Your two sons were fed to a different war
& spit back out. Now

they induct the nervous teenagers of Phoenix
into the intricacies of parallel parking,

the number of feet to trail the car ahead.
You & I are a late-night phone call.

You stretch out beside your drained pool,
shirtless in the heat

with a bottle of Jack. I cradle my California wine.
When your new prosthesis topples

to the cement by the lounge chair
I try to hear

what the fallen man says
as you set him upright.

You Were

the bride of gin, bride
of men you followed home & let fuck you

only to discover that they already had a woman,
a woman who would never know

what you had done with her man, never
know what a shit she was married to, you were

enamored of impulse, tearing flower heads from sidewalk squares
that had converted from cement

to soil. How pure your longing
to be anything other than yourself. How difficult

to extricate the stem, only to hold the scattering,
brooding petals

& how you longed for that stem. Little former whore,
self-you-have-almost-outgrown, think

of Clytia, pining for Apollo, her whole face turned
toward an idea of heaven. Think

of the faces turned toward you now, as you recite
from the myth you have made,

all of them listening
to you. Of all flowers: you.

The First Line Is the Deepest

I have been one acquainted with the spatula,
the slotted, scuffed, Teflon-coated spatula

that lifts a solitary hamburger from pan to plate,
acquainted with the vibrator known as the Pocket Rocket

and the dildo that goes by Tex
and I have gone out, a drunken bitch

in order to ruin
what love I was given,

and also I have measured out
my life in little pills – Zoloft,

Restoril, Celexa,
Xanax.

For I am a poet. It is my job, my duty
to know wherein lies the beauty

of this degraded body,
or maybe

it's the degradation in the beautiful body,
the ugly me

groping back to my desk to piss
on perfection, to lay my kiss

of mortal confusion
upon the mouth of infinite wisdom.

My kiss says razors and pain, my kiss says
America is charged with the madness

of God. Sundays, too,
the soldiers get up early, and put on their fatigues in the blue-

black day. Black milk. Black gold. Texas tea.
Into the valley of Halliburton rides the infantry –

Why does one month have to be the cruelest,
can't they all be equally cruel? I have seen the best

gamers of your generation, joysticking their M1 tanks through
the sewage-filled streets. Whose

world this is I think I know.

Another Day on Earth

(Tsunami, December 26, 2004)

Souls were arriving, souls were departing
amid the usual screaming and crying.
A lot of drinks were being tossed back,
a lot of women were thinking about their hair.
People were loving the quiet as snow fell,
burying the cars. More than one man
was thinking about his penis. Birds were landing
on statues, birds were snapping up insects.
Prisoners were tending invisible flowers in their cells.
A lot of televisions were feeling vaguely spiritual.
A lot of shoes were hurting.
A lot of hearts had fallen from the trees
and were skittering along in the wind.
All the oceans suddenly realised
they were one ocean, whereupon
the Akashic angel whose job it is
to record each moment's folding and unfolding
paused, then went on furiously writing.

The Smallest Town Alive

has one sign:

NOW ENTERING NOW LEAVING

You've passed through & won't
come back. Goodbye,

your life

was so many one-horse stoplights
swaying on wires

in a high wind

a lone dog crossing the street
at an angle

a flurry of porches
you won't remember.

On this one I pose

barefoot in a dress
on the bottom step

an ice chip on my tongue
in my pocket a glowing coal

I am trying to crush
into a name.

The Matter

Some men break your heart in two...
DOROTHY PARKER, 'Experience'

Some men carry you to bed with your boots on.
Some men say your name like a verbal tic.
Some men slap on an emotional surcharge for every erotic encounter.
Some men are slightly mentally ill, and thinking of joining a gym.
Some men have moved on and can't be seduced, even in the dream
    bars where you meet them.
Some men who were younger are now the age you were then.
Some men aren't content with mere breakage, they've got to burn you
    to the ground.
Some men you've reduced to ashes are finally dusting themselves off.
Some men are made of fiberglass.
Some men have deep holes drilled in by a war, you can't fill them.
Some men are delicate and torn.
Some men will steal your bracelet if you let them spend the night.
Some men will want to fuck your poems, and instead they will find
    you.
Some men will say, 'I'd like to see how you look when you come,' and
    then hail a cab.
Some men are a list of ingredients with no recipe.
Some men never see you.
Some men will blindfold you during sex, then secretly put on high heels.
Some men will try on your black fishnet stockings in a hotel in Rome,
    or Saran Wrap you to a bedpost in New Orleans.
Some of these men will be worth trying to keep.
Some men will write obtuse, condescending reviews of your work,
    making you remember these lines by Frank O'Hara:
I cannot possibly think of you / other than you are: the assassin / of my
orchards.
Some men, let's face it, really are too small.
Some men are too large, but it's not usually a deal breaker.
Some men don't have one at all.

Some men will slap you in a way you'll like.
Some men will want to crawl inside you to die.
Some men never clean up the matter.
Some men hand you their hearts like leaflets,
and some men's hearts seem to circle forever: you catch sight of
    them on clear nights,
bright dots among the stars, and wait for their orbits to decay, for
    them to fall to earth.

Crossing

I stash my heart in my boot.
I've got a broken knife for you.
You're not dying for love,
you're not even injured.
Not a scratch, not a nick,
no throb in the bones,
no slight headache
starting behind the eyes.
I'm walking on a dead ocean
all the fish in my body in free fall.
I adore you sinkingly.
You're what. You're whom.
In every room. A dog starts racketing:
it's you. Siren
ratcheting off the blue.
I tie myself to the table.
I bolt myself to the bed.
When the phone's black call comes
I light another silence in my head.

Weaponry

I used an arrow to kill the spider.
I used a steamroller to flatten the worm.

For the ants I called in an air strike.
Bee that found its way in through the screen:

blowtorch.
The mammals were easier –

a bucket of water for submerging the cat,
a poisoned word thrown to the dog.

For love, only a kitchen match. That
and a stove leaking gas

and waiting until the dinner
was good and burned.

Suite pour les amours perdues

1

Needle & groove: Chet Baker
whose voice (someone said) was 'like being

sweet-talked by the void'   – something else
was playing then, but this song's all

nostalgia, so: blues & night   &
a parked truck in a nearly empty lot (&

three, four, & one)   *I fall*
on your lap, too easily, for love to ever

straddling you, face tilted up
bridge & improvise, & then the blank

in the record (*last*):
cease.   Desist.   Lay back and swing.

2

O too-young, & the perfect musculature
of a dumb statue, but you

were clever. & loved Mahler.
After 19 – and his tragedies, his music

became... I forget. Instead,
clean sweat & grapefruit, how you greeted

every dog on the street, puppy,
& how once I knelt, my mouth   fastened

to you, & you moved backwards
slowly   & I followed, on my knees

to Truth –

3

Bottle rockets out the kitchen window
parchment-cooked fish

dark rum, blindfold, Schubert's 'Impromptus'

& the black box that picked up communications
between pilots & the SFO tower –   no one

in this room of memory
but us, dear

one,   & no door
for anyone else to enter, so

in total privacy, we live
in air-

waves, crackling &
                        static.

4

Ah drunk & stumbling with your
guitar & brilliant   when not

drunk &
or using again, *The only time it's all*

all right   Seeing the nothing
that wasn't there

and then it was. *Adieu, adieu*
Quand il me prend dans ses bras

Il me parle tout bas
Je vois in my dreams

5

& last but not,
sweet karmic

valentine: The second time
we slowed it down,   and risked

a dirge. Should we have left
ourselves to memory, where we're always

best –   should we have stitched
it back, or let it rest...

in love too
and later the singer's lovely

wrecked face reflected
in the lid of the closed piano.

In the Lonely Universe

the moon gets up as usual,
heads for the refrigerator or bathroom,
then lies awake, longing for
the Xanax it resembles.
Sex is a fantasy and a spasm.
Music is a slasher movie,
beauty stalked by horror.
Single notes aren't really single;
they're out on the sidewalks sipping lattes
with their flats and sharps,
their invisible naturals.
That song about Galileo and reincarnation
sends you into hysteria
at warp speed.
So do green Toyota trucks,
each with your ex at the wheel.
You open the box with the new lamp
and the packing explodes
into Styroflakes, clinging all over you.
It's white in the lonely universe.
Also, you have to assemble things
following instructions in a language
that doesn't quite exist.
Please rate the last movie you rented
using our system of stars. Upstairs
the newlyweds vacuum late into the night.

Merrily

Keep bailing, keep bailing,
never mind the rain.
What, no bucket? Use your shoe.
Sandals, eh. You've got two hands, man,
don't whine about the manacles
or the snapped-off mast.
List, list.
Row, row, row.

Malice

Oily, wily.
Whip-tailed.

Fairy-handed, reaching in
to skim the soul's fat.

Rat in the mouth of the man
who calls you *nigger*
as we exit the cab.

Making its nest of shreds in my belly
as I scream back.

Whiskered, feverish.
Or maybe winged, maybe

beaked – ravening over the suffering, glad

for the shiny scraps, gleeful.
Self-lovely thrill

of the higher reaches of air –

then getting beyond even pleasure.
Just doing the necessary

work of creating
(mite-riddled, death-mottled)

the hell down there.

Sui

Little beautiful abused,
        cinder scrap caught
                in the updraft –

Needle thief,
        She Who Ironed Her Forearm Black,
                bone-bare (healed now –

nearly). Lovely
        girl burning in a glass,
                wick in a lake

that whitens
        opaque, blade-scored.
                Blued and grieving

you keep moving.
        Every time I open
                the box you gave me,

the little ballerina –
        glittering, indifferent,
                the size of a bullet –

unfolds.
        She stands, poised.
                If I turn the key

she'll turn.
        Trapped on her stage
                with that killing music.

My Heart

That Mississippi chicken shack.
That initial-scarred tabletop,
that tiny little dance floor to the left of the band.
That kiosk at the mall selling caramels and kitsch.
That tollbooth with its white-plastic-gloved worker
handing you your change.
That phone booth with the receiver ripped out.
That dressing room in the fetish boutique,
those curtains and mirrors.
That funhouse, that horror, that soundtrack of screams.
That putti-filled heaven raining gilt from the ceiling.
That haven for truckers, that bottomless cup.
That biome. That wilderness preserve.
That landing strip with no runway lights
where you are aiming your plane,
imagining a voice in the tower,
imagining a tower.

Semper

He says, Here's what men really want: blow job, then fucking, girl on top – or next best, fucking her face down. A fifty-caliber machine gun will take down an aircraft, will damage a tank, and now there's a rifle with a ten-shot magazine, shoulder-fired, for sniping long-distance. My girlfriend quit night-managing the Quik Stop because of all the stress and is looking for something part-time. She'll sneak off to the store and slam down two tall beers so when we go to a party, she can pretend not to be drinking. I put her picture on Dreammates.com and pretended to be her, for a gag. Sometimes late at night I write back to the sad fucks who respond to her profile. I hardly sleep anymore and I still have bad dreams. Being able to sit for hours without moving is what made me a good cop, when I was a cop. My new friend Ray is a cop and lets me ride along once in a while, those are the happiest times I have anymore. When Ray was a sniper in Afghanistan, a pregnant woman got off the bus near the Embassy one day and started spraying with an AK-47, he got a two-for-one. The kid would have just grown up one day and shot everyone. That's how he looked at it. Do you understand what I'm saying? In Vietnam, a kid came running up with a grenade in his hand, you shot that little body and blew it apart. My girlfriend has orgasms that could peel wallpaper. That's something, anyway, he says.

Shrine

Our Lady of dejection, goddess of sleeplessness & dread, of owl-shriek,
of the old man next door hawking up phlegm, his rasp & spit, his
      heavy sigh,

Our Lady of isolate evenings spent sifting for coins in the shipwreck
      at the bottom of a bottle,
Lady of the perforated heart, of errands looming like the labors of
      Hercules,

Lady of consoling, tormenting memories unstoppered from the soul-jar
& spilled shimmering in answer to unanswerable thirst,

I love your downcast eyes, your outstretched hands,
your alcove of fog-light descending from the stratosphere;

I love how you forbear us, how you force our pain to flowering,
unlike God who has forsaken us in favor of those who praise Him,

for I cannot praise Him with my awful strings, with my terrible song,
Lady of wind in the yards

tearing down trees in the dark, Lady of sulfurous rain
& washed-out roads & snapped power lines flailing

& sparking, oh my mother, at your lovely feet I lay my bitter offering.

News

Because no reporters came to my door
wanting to confirm my low opinion
of the Bush administration,

because not even the Jehovah's Witnesses,
who can usually be counted on
to arrive each Saturday

bearing informative articles on Satan's wiles
and the hour of judgment
can be counted on this afternoon,

I have no one to tell
that the load of laundry I managed
to carry to the washer

has been transferred successfully
to the dryer. I even was able
to make myself coffee and toss the cat's toy

onto her carpeted platform
before returning to my bed.
These were little victories

over a sullen god – the one who hunkers down
and rocks back and forth, muttering
that there's no reason to go on

lifting the stone of today
only to watch it roll down into tomorrow.
And now I feel compelled to report

that when the clothes were dry and warm
I got up and folded them and put them away.
Then I finally dressed, late in the afternoon,

and looked out the window and saw
my neighbor, an old black man who lives alone
and sits on his porch most days

in a ratty kitchen chair. So I got my harmonica
and played a bit of Sonny Terry I'd been working on
and I don't know if he listened, if it lit

a match to the damp cigarette of his joy
I can't say, but maybe it did
in some small and unrecorded way.

Happiness After Grief

feels like such a betrayal: the hurt not denied, not pushed away, but gone entirely for that moment you can't help feeling good in, a moment of sudden, irrational joy over nothing of consequence, really, which makes it all somehow seem even worse. Shouldn't happiness be the result of some grand event, something adequate to counter that aching, gaping chasm that opened when... But, no: it's merely this: there goes our little neighbor, running barefoot, no pants, fox stole wrapped around her shoulders.

My Black Angel

BLUES POEMS AND PORTRAITS

(2014)

Cigar Box Banjo

Blind Willie Johnson could coax
music from a single string. God plucked a rib
and found a woman. Concert aria
in the gypsy song, long groan
of orgasm in the first kiss, plastic bag
of heroin ripening in the poppy fields.
Right now, in a deep pocket of a politician's brain,
a bad idea is traveling along an axon
to make sure the future resembles a cobra
rather than an ocarina.
Still there's hope in every cartoon bib
above which a tiny unfinished skull in
its beneficence dispenses a drooling grin.
The heart may be a trashy organ,
but when it plucks its shiny banjo
I see blue wings in the rain.

Creased Map of the Underworld

Nothing is so beautiful as death,
thinks Death: stilled lark on the lawn,
its twiggy legs drawn up, squashed blossoms
of skunks and opossums on the freeway,
dog that drags itself trembling down
the front porch step, and stops
in a black-gummed grimace
before toppling into the poppies.
The ugly poppies. In Afghanistan
they are again made beautiful
by a mysterious blight. Ugly
are the arriving American soldiers, newly shorn
and checking their email,
but beautiful when face-up in the road
or their parts scattered
like bullet- or sprinkler-spray
or stellar remains. Lovely
is the nearly expired star
casting its mass into outer space,
lovelier the supernova
tearing itself apart
or collapsing like Lana Turner
in Frank O'Hara's poem.
Nothing is so beautiful as a poem
except maybe a nightingale,
thinks the poet writing about death,
sinking Lethe-wards. Lovely river
in which the names are carefully entered.
In this quadrant are the rivers of grief and fire.
Grid north. Black azimuth.
Down rivers of *Fuck yous* and orchids
steer lit hearts in little boats
gamely making their way,

spinning and flaming, flaming
and spiraling, always down –
down, the most beautiful of the directions.

Guitar Strings

Six stings
that bright-stain
the air.
Blues sutras
of rain and ruin.
When you hold a guitar
you're truant.
Let the saints and aunts
wait on the stairs
while you sing
smokestacks and satin
and the train
comes raging
past all the signs
to take you to your sins.

Half-Hearted Sonnet

He'd left his belt. She
followed him and
threw it in the street.
Wine: kisses: snake: end

of their story. Be-
gin again, under-
stand what happened; de-
spite that battered

feeling, it will have been
worth it; better to
have etc…
(– *not to have been born*

at all – Schopenhauer.)
But, soft! Enter tears.

Radio Blues

Men wake up drunk, but never on champagne.
They get death letters. They get the jake leg.
They find their guitars and put on their shoes.
If only I could find the door back to you.

Women study evil, but I don't know how.
The crossroads are nothing but a liquor store now.
Everyone wants to dive headfirst into love.
I want to put my hand to a red-hot stove.

Morning and midnight, the voices moan.
I wish you would call me on my toy telephone.
Blues pouring like concrete from a spinning drum.
Before it sets I'm going to lay myself down.

You were the river that drowned me most.
You were. Now it's the radio host
choosing the music, bringing you back –
you, and the door, and the foolproof lock.

Open Mic

Everyone gets a microphone at birth
which is why everyone wails at first,
testing the mortal sound system.
Check one two, check check check
goes the bird mobile over the crib,
the miniature electric train,
the babbling, self-peeing doll which looks
at first like an infant and then
like your mother on her last Thanksgiving.
You feel like you've just stepped onstage
but here comes the wrap-it-up music,
the MC slitting his throat with his finger.
Next up is the fat chanteuse
who sounds like a gerbil
trying to produce an aria
while clenched in the mouth of a housecat.
Meanwhile, the wasted young
in one another's arms,
drinking endless pints of cheap beer
but mostly spilling it on each other
because to gesture is to slosh,
and the young are full of gestures,
Meet my friend and *Fuck off*
and *Let's go outside to get high,*
which they do, standing close together
in the doorway of the showroom
for discount medical equipment.
Meanwhile, the house band performs
for a few spastic dancers.
Your bar stool is bolted to the floor.
Your lonely, twitchy heart
lunges like a dog on a chain,

only dimly understanding the reason
it must exhaust itself
and then begin to howl,
though no one ever comes.

Heraclitean

In goes the cafeteria worker in her hairnet.
In goes the philosophy teacher
explaining the theory of eternal
return, and Anton Stadler with his clarinet,
still owing money to Mozart. In
goes Mozart. Everyone flopped into the creel
of the happy fisherman, everyone eaten.
Every river is Lethean,
so why should we care
if it's not the same river? I hate
how everything changes, tree
to failing term paper, chatelaine
to beheaded plotter, drug dealer to narc.
The heart softening faster than cereal
but then hardening to a relic
which turns into another line
of depressed poetry to recite
to the next eager trainee
anxious to be more than lint.
Going up, you're also going down, so either
way, as your mother said, *Be nice.*
When she went in, she was very thin.
Earth, air, fire, water, mother.
Fish pulse slowly under the river ice.

Queen of the Game

Show me a man what will love me till I die
GWENDOLYN BROOKS, 'Queen of the Blues'

The reveal. The tell. The way you show
what you don't mean to. As for me –
I'll never let you know. I've a veil. A caul. A
heavy theater curtain. I can fool a man
across a room into thinking he's inside me. What
the blues taught me is pleasure won't abide. Some will
say it's otherwise. They'll lay down their cards for love
and go all in. They'll walk away with nothing, but not me.
I'm in it for the win. What I hide, I'll hide till
hell closes down and the river's dark eye
is done with tears. Dry and alone is how I'll die.

Harmonica

Traaain goin north, sang Noah
Lewis, father unknown, who'd charm
Satan from a woodpile with his horn.
He could play two harps at once. Cain
and Abel, from his nose and mouth. Play that Iron
Horse, though he never left the south. Cold rain,
cold end: frostbite and gangrene, no choir
to carry him from poverty, the blues gone minor.
Busked, stomped and sang. Couldn't keep him from harm.
The spirit burns away; what's left is char,
until someone pulls up a kitchen chair
and starts in on 'Chickasaw Special'. No
tears for Noah Lewis. Moan
and sing *Take a woman from another man*
and bang like holy hell on a coal-oil can.

Please

I was cruel but you were cruel first,
cried the rose to its thorn
before sending it away,
then making dinner alone
and toppling into a wine glass,
falling into bed with petals askew.
Love is a bluebird from hell.
Love is a teacup Chihuahua.
I love you means my mouth is full
of darkling beetle grubs
and if I fall off your lap I may die.
I'm sorry love isn't a flower.
I'm sorry my heart is a sinkhole.
It swallowed a freezer once.
You were right to go. But come back.
Cried the rose. Coughing up
a few thawing pork chops.

Penis Blues

I miss the penis.
I feel like a word with no vowels;
no one wants to pronounce me.

Woke up this morning,
looked around for my penis.
J'ai été dévasté;

le zizi, Je ne pouvais pas le trouver.
I would like to order a penis, please,
with dressing on the side.

Also, this soup could use a dash of penis.
Señor Plátano: ¿dónde estás?
Mr Defile Me, where you at?

There's something lacking in the décor:
an artfully placed penis.
There used to be one, right over there.

Reading the paper, using a drill gun,
leaving socks on the floor.
Now there's a hole in my heart,

penis-sized. Ohhhhh prostate
baby you up and gone.
Those ol' seminal vesicles done rambled on.

Corpus cavernosum, *mm-ahhh – hmm*
mmmmmmmmmmmmmmmmmmmmmm
hmmmm-ummm-ohhh-mmmmmmmm.

A penis has taken flight.
Probably gon' fly all night.
There's a flock of penises headed south.

Their cries recede over the distant car dealerships,
over the darkened pleather interiors
and the stoned janitor, slopping his mop

in a bucket of dirty water.

Spell Against Impermanence

Faeries, gryphons, wrens, blue roses.
Cartoon girls in impish poses.

Isis. Sanskrit text. Chinese.
Snake eyes. Marijuana leaves.

Skulls. Knives. Hellhounds. Scorpions.
Tygers. Harpies. Gangrened demons.

Lover leave and child abort.
Brother's liver dredge in dirt.

Steep in piss and shit and pain
Father's corpse and mother's brain.

Fire feed, and ash inhale –
Heart lash to the breaking wheel –

Lightning. Lotus. Chameleon.
Slide the needle deeper in.

Black Snake Blues

I'm tired of dragging a man's name
like a stick along fence slats

and the song always broken
and the light always asking me for money.

Let me lie down where the roads cross.

oh black snake crawlin'

I'll scatter my powders and salt
and wait for the rider

with a bottle of whiskey
and another of graveyard dirt.

crawlin' in my room

I'll wait
while the heat seethes up and becomes

pure silence for miles
in all twelve directions.

I'll watch for a wild horse, a storm.

Let me wait for the sky to bear down
and tell me who it wants,

oh black snake crawlin'

let it want some other woman,
let it find her and hold the night open.

Northeast Corridor Blues

Lost my ticket when I got on the train
Conductor said sorry you got to pay again
If he was a rock I'd be a speck of sand

Passing yards of junked cars, their hoods popped open
Water towers trailer parks local taverns
Gone as soon as you look at them

Traveling down to DC to bury my mother
Put her ashes next to the bones of my father
Tell the priest he won't have to bother

Everyone's a stone but I'm a speck of sand
No matter what I do I've got to pay again
Lost my ticket when I got on the train

When Joe Filisko Plays the Blues

cotton claps & shouts in every Georgia field
& the hounds are set loose to run down the fox

they will forever never catch.
He can play a front porch on a rundown shack

where a man is singing his hurt
like pressing a thumb on a bruise,

probably it's shaped like a woman
or a few years in prison.

You can ride those blues all the way to Chicago
where the lake swallows snowmelt

& turns bitter with whiskey.
That's the kind of blues he plays.

The kind where a muddy cloud
looks like a train. The kind where a train

looks like a trip to Paris, & Paris
is a woman wearing nothing but jewels,

& you have to know her but never will.
Go back home, follow the high notes down.

Joe will take you all the way underground.
He'll fill your mouth with dirt

& convince you it's barbeque.
He'll lay those blues down on you.

If you meet the devil, tell him Filisko
sent you – he'll let you go.

If you meet an angel, hold on hard
& don't ever let her meet Joe.

Salvation

I am a mote.
I fade to insignificance daily.
At least I'm a part of something.
An extremely tiny part.
I sing in the mote-choir, naked and ruined.
In the lamplight I drift over the page.
In the produce aisle, I'm the slow hiss
of mist over the broccoli.
I am a paramecium of the imagination.
I am a bindi on the third eye of a dust bunny.
An immigrant with a rag is my destroyer.
Among the motes of rain I descend.
But so do you.
Even God is a mote,
adored by other motes.
I shall lift up mine eyes to the clouds.
Who among you will be my love-specks?
Soon we shall seep.
Deep in the earth, the undone motes.
Look, the ashes we scattered
are sparking on the sea.

The Women

We turn sixteen. We cannabis
and Vicodin. We Dexadrine.

We stolen scarves and dresses
disordered in boys' cars

and falling down on dance floors.
We waste years and wishes

and finally marry
or wait for a king who does dishes.

We curse bosses.
We birth give and bring forth

and feel our unworth.
We divorce. We grow

uncool. We carpool.
We forgive those who lie down against us.

We lose June. We lose July.
In August we look in mirrors and want to die.

We hot flash. We worry cash.
Night cream lotus jewel and bicep curl

we try. We buy high heels.
We lunch. We find lumps.

We put our feet in the stirrups
and our lives in the hands

and our hearts to the wheel
which grinds us,

and so
over time

we polish to a hard shine
and we divine.

Wine Tasting

I think I detect cracked leather.
I'm pretty certain I smell the cherries
from a Shirley Temple my father bought me

in 1959, in a bar in Orlando, Florida,
and the chlorine from my mother's bathing cap.
And last winter's kisses, like salt on black ice,

like the moon slung away from the earth.
When Li Po drank wine, the moon dove
in the river, and he staggered after.

Probably he tasted laughter.
When my friend Susan drinks
she cries because she's Irish

and childless. I'd like to taste,
one more time, the rain that arrived
one afternoon and fell just short

of where I stood, so I leaned my face in,
alive in both worlds at once,
knowing it would end and not caring.